United States Government Accountability Office

GAO

By the Comptroller General of the United States

December 2011

Government Auditing Standards

2011 Revision

GAO-12-331G

United States Government Accountability Office

By the Comptroller General of the United States

GAO

December 2011

Government Auditing Standards

2011 Revision

U.S. Government Accountability Office

GAO 90 YEARS 1921-2011
ACCOUNTABILITY ★ INTEGRITY ★ RELIABILITY

GAO-12-331G

Contents

Chapter 5
Standards for
Attestation
Engagements

Chapter 6
Field Work
Standards for
Performance
Audits

Chapter 7 Reporting Standards for Performance Audits		

Appendixes

Index

Contents

Abbreviations

AICPA	American Institute of Certified Public Accountants
AU-C	AICPA *Codification of Statements on Auditing Standards for Auditing*
AT	AICPA *Codification of Statements on Standards for Attestation Engagements*
CPA	certified public accountants
CPE	continuing professional education
COSO	Committee of Sponsoring Organizations of the Treadway Commission
ERISA	Employee Retirement Income Security Act
FISCAM	*Federal Information System Controls Audit Manual*
GAAP	generally accepted accounting principles
GAGAS	generally accepted government auditing standards
GAO	Government Accountability Office
IT	information technology
IAASB	International Auditing and Assurance Standards Board
IIA	Institute of Internal Auditors
ISAE	International Standards on Assurance Engagements
ISA	International Standards on Auditing
MD&A	management's discussion and analysis
OMB	Office of Management and Budget
PCAOB	Public Company Accounting Oversight Board
SAS	Statements on Auditing Standards
SSAE	Statements on Standards for Attestation Engagements

G A O
Accountability • Integrity • Reliability

United States Government Accountability Office
Washington, D.C. 20548

Comptroller General
of the United States

Audits provide essential accountability and transparency over government programs. Given the current challenges facing governments and their programs, the oversight provided through auditing is more critical than ever. Government auditing provides objective analysis and information needed to make the decisions necessary to help create a better future. The professional standards presented in this 2011 revision of Government Auditing Standards provide a framework for performing high-quality audit work with competence, integrity, objectivity, and independence to provide accountability and to help improve government operations and services. These standards provide the foundation for government auditors to lead by example in the areas of independence, transparency, accountability, and quality through the audit process.

The 2011 revision of Government Auditing Standards represents a modernized version of the standards, taking into account recent changes in other auditing standards, including international standards. This revision supersedes the 2007 revision. It contains the following major changes from the 2007 revision that reinforce the principles of transparency and accountability and provide the framework for high-quality government audits that add value.

- A conceptual framework for independence was added to provide a means for auditors to assess their independence for activities that are not expressly prohibited in the standards. This more principles-based approach to analyzing independence provides the framework for auditors to assess the unique facts and circumstances that arise during their work.

- This revision drops discussion surrounding certain AICPA Statements on Auditing Standards (SAS) and

Statements on Standards for Attestation
Engagements (SSAE) requirements that were
incorporated by reference and included in the 2007
revision, as the standards have converged in those
areas.

- The definition of validity as an aspect of the quality
  of evidence has been clarified for performance
  audits.

Effective with the implementation dates for the 2011
revision of Government Auditing Standards, GAO is
also retiring Government Auditing Standards: Answers
to Independence Standard Questions (GAO-02-870G,
July 2002).

This revision of the standards has gone through an
extensive deliberative process, including public
comments and input from the Comptroller General's
Advisory Council on Government Auditing Standards.
The Advisory Council generally consists of about 25
experts in financial and performance auditing and
reporting drawn from federal, state, and local
government; the private sector; and academia. The
views of all parties were thoroughly considered in
finalizing the standards.

The 2011 revision of Government Auditing Standards
will be effective for financial audits and attestation
engagements for periods ending on or after December
15, 2012, and for performance audits beginning on or
after December 15, 2011. Early implementation is not
permitted.

An electronic version of this document and any
interpretive publications can be accessed at
http://www.gao.gov/yellowbook.

I extend special thanks to the members of the Advisory Council for their extensive input and feedback through the entire process of developing and finalizing the standards.

Gene L. Dodaro
Comptroller General
of the United States

December 2011

Chapter 1

Government Auditing: Foundation and Ethical Principles

Introduction

1.01 The concept of accountability for use of public resources and government authority is key to our nation's governing processes. Management and officials entrusted with public resources are responsible for carrying out public functions and providing service to the public effectively, efficiently, economically, ethically, and equitably within the context of the statutory boundaries of the specific government program.

1.02 As reflected in applicable laws, regulations, agreements, and standards, management and officials of government programs are responsible for providing reliable, useful, and timely information for transparency and accountability of these programs and their operations.[1] Legislators, oversight bodies, those charged with governance,[2] and the public need to know whether (1) management and officials manage government resources and use their authority properly and in compliance with laws and regulations; (2) government programs are achieving their objectives and desired outcomes; and (3) government services are provided effectively, efficiently, economically, ethically, and equitably.

1.03 Government auditing is essential in providing accountability to legislators, oversight bodies, those charged with governance, and the public. Audits[3] provide an independent, objective, nonpartisan assessment of the stewardship, performance, or cost of government policies, programs, or operations, depending upon the type and scope of the audit.

---

[1] See paragraph A1.08 for additional information on management's responsibilities.

[2] See paragraphs A1.05 through A1.07 for additional discussion on the role of those charged with governance.

[3] See paragraph 1.07c for discussion of the term "audit" as it is used in chapters 1 through 3 and corresponding sections of the Appendix.

Purpose and Applicability of GAGAS

1.04 The professional standards and guidance contained in this document, commonly referred to as generally accepted government auditing standards (GAGAS), provide a framework for conducting high quality audits with competence, integrity, objectivity, and independence. These standards are for use by auditors of government entities and entities that receive government awards and audit organizations performing GAGAS audits. Overall, GAGAS contains standards for audits, which are comprised of individual requirements that are identified by terminology as discussed in paragraphs 2.14 through 2.18. GAGAS contains requirements and guidance dealing with ethics, independence, auditors' professional judgment and competence, quality control, performance of the audit, and reporting.

1.05 Audits performed in accordance with GAGAS provide information used for oversight, accountability, transparency, and improvements of government programs and operations. GAGAS contains requirements and guidance to assist auditors in objectively acquiring and evaluating sufficient, appropriate evidence and reporting the results. When auditors perform their work in this manner and comply with GAGAS in reporting the results, their work can lead to improved government management, better decision making and oversight, effective and efficient operations, and accountability and transparency for resources and results.

1.06 Provisions of laws, regulations, contracts, grant agreements, or policies frequently require audits be conducted in accordance with GAGAS. In addition, many auditors and audit organizations voluntarily choose to perform their work in accordance with GAGAS. The requirements and guidance in GAGAS apply to audits of government entities, programs, activities, and functions, and of government assistance administered by contractors, nonprofit entities, and other nongovernmental entities when the use of GAGAS is required or is voluntarily followed.[4]

1.07 This paragraph describes the use of the following terms in GAGAS.

a. The term "auditor" as it is used throughout GAGAS describes individuals performing work in accordance with GAGAS (including audits and attestation engagements) regardless of job title. Therefore, individuals who may have the titles auditor, analyst, practitioner, evaluator, inspector, or other similar titles are considered auditors in GAGAS.

b. The term "audit organization" as it is used throughout GAGAS refers to government audit organizations as well as public accounting or other firms that perform audits and attestation engagements using GAGAS.

c. The term "audit" as it is used in chapters 1 through 3 and corresponding sections of the Appendix refers to financial audits, attestation engagements, and performance audits conducted in accordance with GAGAS.

---

[4]See paragraphs A1.02 through A1.04 for discussion of laws, regulations, and guidelines that require use of GAGAS.

1.08 A government audit organization can be structurally located within or outside the audited entity.[5] Audit organizations that are external to the audited entity and report to third parties are considered to be external audit organizations. Audit organizations that are accountable to senior management and those charged with governance of the audited entity, and do not generally issue their reports to third parties external to the audited entity, are considered internal audit organizations.

1.09 Some government audit organizations represent a unique hybrid of external auditing and internal auditing in their oversight role for the entities they audit. These audit organizations have external reporting requirements consistent with the reporting requirements for external auditors while at the same time being part of their respective agencies. These audit organizations often have a dual reporting responsibility to their legislative body as well as to the agency head and management.

Ethical Principles

1.10 The ethical principles presented in this section provide the foundation, discipline, and structure, as well as the climate that influence the application of GAGAS. This section sets forth fundamental principles rather than establishing specific standards or requirements.

1.11 Because auditing is essential to government accountability to the public, the public expects audit organizations and auditors who conduct their work in accordance with GAGAS to follow ethical principles. Management of the audit organization sets the tone for

---

[5]See paragraph 1.19 for a discussion of objectivity and paragraphs 3.27 through 3.32 for requirements related to independence considerations for government auditors and audit organization structure.

ethical behavior throughout the organization by maintaining an ethical culture, clearly communicating acceptable behavior and expectations to each employee, and creating an environment that reinforces and encourages ethical behavior throughout all levels of the organization. The ethical tone maintained and demonstrated by management and staff is an essential element of a positive ethical environment for the audit organization.

1.12 Conducting audit work in accordance with ethical principles is a matter of personal and organizational responsibility. Ethical principles apply in preserving auditor independence,[6] taking on only work that the audit organization is competent[7] to perform, performing high-quality work, and following the applicable standards cited in the auditors' report. Integrity and objectivity are maintained when auditors perform their work and make decisions that are consistent with the broader interest of those relying on the auditors' report, including the public.

1.13 Other ethical requirements or codes of professional conduct may also be applicable to auditors who conduct audits in accordance with GAGAS. For example, individual auditors who are members of professional organizations or are licensed or certified professionals may also be subject to ethical requirements of those professional organizations or licensing bodies. Auditors employed by government entities may also be subject to government ethics laws and regulations.

---

[6]See paragraphs 3.02 through 3.59 for requirements related to independence.

[7]See paragraphs 3.69 through 3.81 for additional information on competence.

1.14 The ethical principles that guide the work of auditors who conduct audits in accordance with GAGAS are

a. the public interest;

b. integrity;

c. objectivity;

d. proper use of government information, resources, and positions; and

e. professional behavior.

The Public Interest

1.15 The public interest is defined as the collective well-being of the community of people and entities the auditors serve. Observing integrity, objectivity, and independence in discharging their professional responsibilities assists auditors in meeting the principle of serving the public interest and honoring the public trust. The principle of the public interest is fundamental to the responsibilities of auditors and critical in the government environment.

1.16 A distinguishing mark of an auditor is acceptance of responsibility to serve the public interest. This responsibility is critical when auditing in the government environment. GAGAS embodies the concept of accountability for public resources, which is fundamental to serving the public interest.

Integrity

1.17 Public confidence in government is maintained and strengthened by auditors performing their professional responsibilities with integrity. Integrity includes auditors conducting their work with an attitude that is objective, fact-based, nonpartisan, and nonideological with regard to audited entities and users of the auditors' reports. Within the constraints of applicable confidentiality laws, rules, or policies, communications with the audited entity, those charged with governance, and the individuals contracting for or requesting the audit are expected to be honest, candid, and constructive.

1.18 Making decisions consistent with the public interest of the program or activity under audit is an important part of the principle of integrity. In discharging their professional responsibilities, auditors may encounter conflicting pressures from management of the audited entity, various levels of government, and other likely users. Auditors may also encounter pressures to inappropriately achieve personal or organizational gain. In resolving those conflicts and pressures, acting with integrity means that auditors place priority on their responsibilities to the public interest.

Objectivity

1.19 The credibility of auditing in the government sector is based on auditors' objectivity in discharging their professional responsibilities. Objectivity includes independence of mind and appearance when providing audits, maintaining an attitude of impartiality, having intellectual honesty, and being free of conflicts of interest. Maintaining objectivity includes a continuing assessment of relationships with audited entities and other stakeholders in the context of the auditors' responsibility to the public. The concepts of objectivity and independence are closely related. Independence impairments impact objectivity.[8]

---

[8]See independence standards at paragraphs 3.02 through 3.59.

Proper Use of Government Information, Resources, and Positions

1.20 Government information, resources, and positions are to be used for official purposes and not inappropriately for the auditor's personal gain or in a manner contrary to law or detrimental to the legitimate interests of the audited entity or the audit organization. This concept includes the proper handling of sensitive or classified information or resources.

1.21 In the government environment, the public's right to the transparency of government information has to be balanced with the proper use of that information. In addition, many government programs are subject to laws and regulations dealing with the disclosure of information. To accomplish this balance, exercising discretion in the use of information acquired in the course of auditors' duties is an important part in achieving this goal. Improperly disclosing any such information to third parties is not an acceptable practice.

1.22 Accountability to the public for the proper use and prudent management of government resources is an essential part of auditors' responsibilities. Protecting and conserving government resources and using them appropriately for authorized activities is an important element in the public's expectations for auditors.

1.23 Misusing the position of an auditor for financial gain or other benefits violates an auditor's fundamental responsibilities. An auditor's credibility can be damaged by actions that could be perceived by an objective third party with knowledge of the relevant information as improperly benefiting an auditor's personal financial interests or those of an immediate or close family member; a general partner; an organization for which the auditor serves as an officer, director, trustee, or employee; or an organization with which the auditor is negotiating concerning future employment.

Professional
Behavior

1.24 High expectations for the auditing profession include compliance with all relevant legal, regulatory, and professional obligations and avoidance of any conduct that might bring discredit to auditors' work, including actions that would cause an objective third party with knowledge of the relevant information to conclude that the auditors' work was professionally deficient. Professional behavior includes auditors putting forth an honest effort in performance of their duties and professional services in accordance with the relevant technical and professional standards.

Chapter 2

Standards for Use and Application of GAGAS

| Introduction | **2.01** This chapter establishes requirements and provides guidance for audits[9] performed in accordance with generally accepted government auditing standards (GAGAS). This chapter also identifies the types of audits that may be performed in accordance with GAGAS, explains the terminology that GAGAS uses to identify requirements, explains the relationship between GAGAS and other professional standards, and provides requirements for stating compliance with GAGAS in the auditors' report. |

| Types of GAGAS Audits and Attestation Engagements | **2.02** This section describes the types of audits that audit organizations may perform in accordance with GAGAS. This description is not intended to limit or require the types of audits that may be performed in accordance with GAGAS. |

2.03 All audits begin with objectives, and those objectives determine the type of audit to be performed and the applicable standards to be followed. The types of audits that are covered by GAGAS, as defined by their objectives, are classified in this document as financial audits, attestation engagements, and performance audits.

2.04 In some audits, the standards applicable to the specific objective will be apparent. For example, if the objective is to express an opinion on financial statements, the standards for financial audits apply. However, some audits may have multiple or overlapping objectives. For example, if the objectives are to determine the reliability of performance measures, this work can be done in accordance with either the standards for attestation engagements or performance

---

[9]See paragraph 1.07c for discussion of the term "audit" as it is used in chapters 1 through 3 and corresponding sections of the Appendix.

audits. In cases in which there is a choice between applicable standards, auditors should evaluate users' needs and the auditors' knowledge, skills, and experience in deciding which standards to follow.

2.05 GAGAS requirements apply to the types of audits that may be performed in accordance with GAGAS as follows:

a. Financial audits: the requirements and guidance in chapters 1 through 4 apply.

b. Attestation engagements: the requirements and guidance in chapters 1 through 3, and 5 apply.

c. Performance audits: the requirements and guidance in chapters 1 through 3, 6, and 7 apply.

2.06 Appendix I includes supplemental guidance for auditors and audited entities to assist in the implementation of GAGAS. Appendix I does not establish auditor requirements but instead is intended to facilitate implementation of the standards contained in chapters 2 through 7. Appendix II includes a flowchart which may assist in the application of the conceptual framework for independence.[10]

Financial Audits

2.07 Financial audits provide an independent assessment of whether an entity's reported financial information (e.g., financial condition, results, and use of resources) are presented fairly in accordance with recognized criteria. Financial audits performed in accordance with GAGAS include financial statement audits and other related financial audits:

---

[10]See paragraphs 3.07 through 3.32 for discussion of the conceptual framework.

a. Financial statement audits: The primary purpose of a financial statement audit is to provide an opinion about whether an entity's financial statements are presented fairly in all material respects in conformity with an applicable financial reporting framework. Reporting on financial statement audits performed in accordance with GAGAS also includes reports on internal control over financial reporting and on compliance with provisions of laws, regulations, contracts, and grant agreements that have a material effect on the financial statements.

b. Other types of financial audits: Other types of financial audits conducted in accordance with GAGAS entail various scopes of work, including: (1) obtaining sufficient, appropriate evidence to form an opinion on single financial statements, specified elements, accounts, or items of a financial statement;[11] (2) issuing letters for underwriters and certain other requesting parties;[12] and (3) auditing compliance with applicable compliance requirements relating to one or more government programs.[13]

2.08 GAGAS incorporates by reference the American Institute of Certified Public Accountants (AICPA)

---

[11]See American Institute of Certified Public Accountants (AICPA) *Codification of Statements on Auditing Standards* for Auditing (AU-C) Section 805, *Special Considerations – Audits of Single Financial Statements and Specific Elements, Accounts, or Items of a Financial Statement.*

[12]See AICPA AU-C Section 920, *Letters for Underwriters and Certain Other Requesting Parties.*

[13]See AICPA AU-C Section 935, *Compliance Audits.*

Statements on Auditing Standards (SAS).[14] Additional
requirements for performing financial audits in
accordance with GAGAS are contained in chapter 4.
For financial audits performed in accordance with
GAGAS, auditors should also comply with chapters
1 through 3.

Attestation Engagements

2.09 Attestation engagements can cover a broad range
of financial or nonfinancial objectives about the subject
matter or assertion depending on the users' needs.[15]
GAGAS incorporates by reference the AICPA's
Statements on Standards for Attestation Engagements
(SSAE).[16] Additional requirements for performing
attestation engagements in accordance with GAGAS
are contained in chapter 5. The AICPA's standards
recognize attestation engagements that result in an
examination, a review, or an agreed-upon procedures
report on a subject matter or on an assertion about a
subject matter that is the responsibility of another
party.[17] The three types of attestation engagements are:

a. Examination: Consists of obtaining sufficient,
appropriate evidence to express an opinion on whether
the subject matter is based on (or in conformity with) the

---

[14]See AICPA *Codification of Statements on Auditing Standards* and
paragraph 2.20 for additional discussion on the relationship between
GAGAS and other professional standards. References to the AICPA
Codification of Statements on Auditing Standards use an "AU-C"
identifier to refer to the clarified SASs instead of an "AU" identifier.
"AU-C" is a temporary identifier to avoid confusion with references to
existing "AU" sections, which remain effective through 2013. The "AU-
C" identifier will revert to "AU" in 2014 AICPA *Codification of
Statements on Auditing Standards*, by which time the clarified SASs
become fully effective for all engagements.

[15]See A2.01 for examples of objectives for attestation engagements.

[16]See the AICPA *Codification of Statements on Standards for
Attestation Engagements* (AT) Sections.

[17]See AICPA AT Section 101, *Attest Engagements* and AT Section
201, *Agreed-Upon Procedures Engagements*.

criteria in all material respects or the assertion is presented (or fairly stated), in all material respects, based on the criteria.

b. Review: Consists of sufficient testing to express a conclusion about whether any information came to the auditors' attention on the basis of the work performed that indicates the subject matter is not based on (or not in conformity with) the criteria or the assertion is not presented (or not fairly stated) in all material respects based on the criteria. Auditors should not perform review-level work for reporting on internal control or compliance with provisions of laws and regulations.[18]

c. Agreed-Upon Procedures: Consists of auditors performing specific procedures on the subject matter and issuing a report of findings based on the agreed-upon procedures. In an agreed-upon procedures engagement, the auditor does not express an opinion or conclusion, but only reports on agreed-upon procedures in the form of procedures and findings related to the specific procedures applied.

Performance Audits

2.10 Performance audits are defined as audits that provide findings or conclusions based on an evaluation of sufficient, appropriate evidence against criteria.[19] Performance audits provide objective analysis to assist management and those charged with governance and oversight in using the information to improve program performance and operations, reduce costs, facilitate decision making by parties with responsibility to oversee or initiate corrective action, and contribute to public accountability. The term "program" is used in

---

[18]See AICPA AT Sections 501, *Reporting on an Entity's Internal Control Over Financial Reporting* and 601, *Compliance Attestation.*

[19]See paragraphs 6.37 and A6.02 for discussion of criteria.

GAGAS to include government entities, organizations, programs, activities, and functions.

2.11 Performance audit objectives vary widely and include assessments of program effectiveness, economy, and efficiency; internal control; compliance; and prospective analyses. These overall objectives are not mutually exclusive. Thus, a performance audit may have more than one overall objective. For example, a performance audit with an objective of determining or evaluating program effectiveness may also involve an additional objective of evaluating internal controls to determine the reasons for a program's lack of effectiveness or how effectiveness can be improved. Examples of the various types of the performance audit objectives discussed below are included in Appendix I.[20]

a. Program effectiveness and results audit objectives are frequently interrelated with economy and efficiency objectives. Audit objectives that focus on program effectiveness and results typically measure the extent to which a program is achieving its goals and objectives. Audit objectives that focus on economy and efficiency address the costs and resources used to achieve program results.

b. Internal control audit objectives relate to an assessment of one or more components of an organization's system of internal control that is designed to provide reasonable assurance of achieving effective and efficient operations, reliable financial and performance reporting, or compliance with applicable laws and regulations. Internal control objectives also may be relevant when determining the cause of unsatisfactory program performance. Internal control

---

[20]See paragraphs A2.02 through A2.05 for discussion of performance audit objectives.

comprises the plans, policies, methods, and procedures used to meet the organization's mission, goals, and objectives. Internal control includes the processes and procedures for planning, organizing, directing, and controlling program operations, and management's system for measuring, reporting, and monitoring program performance.[21]

c. Compliance audit objectives relate to an assessment of compliance with criteria established by provisions of laws, regulations, contracts, or grant agreements, or other requirements that could affect the acquisition, protection, use, and disposition of the entity's resources and the quantity, quality, timeliness, and cost of services the entity produces and delivers. Compliance requirements can be either financial or nonfinancial.

d. Prospective analysis audit objectives provide analysis or conclusions about information that is based on assumptions about events that may occur in the future, along with possible actions that the entity may take in response to the future events.

Nonaudit Services Provided by Audit Organizations

2.12 GAGAS does not cover nonaudit services, which are defined as professional services other than audits or attestation engagements. Therefore, auditors do not report that the nonaudit services were conducted in accordance with GAGAS. When performing nonaudit services for an entity for which the audit organization performs a GAGAS audit, audit organizations should communicate with requestors and those charged with governance to clarify that the work performed does not constitute an audit conducted in accordance with GAGAS.

---

[21]See paragraphs A.03 through A.04 for additional discussion of internal control.

2.13 When audit organizations provide nonaudit services to entities for which they also provide GAGAS audits, they should assess the impact that providing those nonaudit services may have on auditor and audit organization independence and respond to any identified threats to independence in accordance with the GAGAS independence standard.[22]

Use of Terminology to Define GAGAS Requirements

2.14 GAGAS contains requirements together with related guidance in the form of application and other explanatory material. The terminology is consistent with the terminology defined in the AICPA's *Codification of Statements on Auditing Standards*.[23] Auditors have a responsibility to consider the entire text of GAGAS in carrying out their work and in understanding and applying the requirements in GAGAS. Not every paragraph of GAGAS carries a requirement that auditors and audit organizations are expected to fulfill. Rather, the requirements are identified through use of specific language.

2.15 GAGAS uses two categories of requirements, identified by specific terms, to describe the degree of responsibility they impose on auditors and audit organizations, as follows:

a. Unconditional requirements: Auditors and audit organizations must comply with an unconditional requirement in all cases where such requirement is relevant. GAGAS uses the word *must* to indicate an unconditional requirement.

---

[22]See paragraphs 3.02 through 3.59 for the GAGAS independence standard.

[23]See AICPA AU-C Section 200, *Overall Objectives of the Independent Auditor and the Conduct of an Audit in Accordance With Generally Accepted Auditing Standards.*

b. Presumptively mandatory requirements: Auditors and audit organizations must comply with a presumptively mandatory requirement in all cases where such a requirement is relevant except in rare circumstances discussed in paragraph 2.16. GAGAS uses the word *should* to indicate a presumptively mandatory requirement.[24]

2.16 In rare circumstances, auditors and audit organizations may determine it necessary to depart from a relevant presumptively mandatory requirement. In such rare circumstances, auditors should perform alternative procedures to achieve the intent of that requirement. The need for the auditors to depart from a relevant presumptively mandatory requirement is expected to arise only when the requirement is for a specific procedure to be performed and, in the specific circumstances of the audit, that procedure would be ineffective in achieving the intent of the requirement. If, in rare circumstances, auditors judge it necessary to depart from a relevant presumptively mandatory requirement, they must document their justification for the departure and how the alternative procedures performed in the circumstances were sufficient to achieve the intent of that requirement.

2.17 In addition to requirements as identified in paragraph 2.15, GAGAS contains related guidance in the form of application and other explanatory material. The application and other explanatory material provides further explanation of the requirements and guidance for carrying them out. In particular, it may explain more precisely what a requirement means or is intended to cover or include examples of procedures that may be appropriate in the circumstances. Although such guidance does not in itself impose a requirement, it is

---

[24]See paragraph 2.25 for additional documentation requirements for departures from GAGAS requirements.

relevant to the proper application of the requirements. Auditors should have an understanding of the application and other explanatory material; how auditors apply the guidance in the audit depends on the exercise of professional judgment in the circumstances consistent with the objective of the requirement. The words "may," "might," and "could" are used to describe these actions and procedures. The application and other explanatory material may also provide background information on matters addressed in GAGAS.

2.18 Auditors also use "interpretive publications" in planning and performing GAGAS audits. Interpretive publications are recommendations on the application of GAGAS in specific circumstances, including audits for entities in specialized industries. Interpretive publications, such as related GAGAS guidance documents and interpretations, are issued under the authority of the Government Accountability Office (GAO) to provide additional guidance on the application of GAGAS.[25] Interpretive publications are not auditing standards, but have the same level of authority as application and other explanatory material in GAGAS.

Relationship between GAGAS and Other Professional Standards

2.19 Auditors may use GAGAS in conjunction with professional standards issued by other authoritative bodies.

2.20 The relationship between GAGAS and other professional standards for financial audits and attestation engagements is as follows:

---

[25]See http://www.gao.gov/yellowbook for a listing of related GAGAS interpretive publications.

a. The AICPA has established professional standards that apply to financial audits and attestation engagements for nonissuers (entities other than issuers[26] under the Sarbanes-Oxley Act of 2002, such as privately held companies, nonprofit entities, and government entities) performed by certified public accountants (CPA). For financial audits and attestation engagements, GAGAS incorporates by reference AICPA standards, as discussed in paragraph 2.08.

b. The International Auditing and Assurance Standards Board (IAASB) has established professional standards that apply to financial audits and assurance engagements. Auditors may elect to use the IAASB standards and the related International Standards on Auditing (ISA) and International Standards on Assurance Engagements (ISAE) in conjunction with GAGAS.

c. The Public Company Accounting Oversight Board (PCAOB) has established professional standards that apply to financial audits and attestation engagements for issuers (generally, publicly traded companies with a reporting obligation under the Securities Exchange Act of 1934). Auditors may elect to use the PCAOB standards in conjunction with GAGAS.

2.21 For performance audits, GAGAS does not incorporate other standards by reference, but recognizes that auditors may use or may be required to use other professional standards in conjunction with GAGAS, such as the following:

---

[26]See the Sarbanes-Oxley Act of 2002 (Public Law 107-204) for discussion of issuers.

a. *International Standards for the Professional Practice of Internal Auditing,* The Institute of Internal Auditors, Inc.;

b. *Guiding Principles for Evaluators,* American Evaluation Association;

c. *The Program Evaluation Standards,* Joint Committee on Standards for Education Evaluation;

d. *Standards for Educational and Psychological Testing,* American Psychological Association; and

e. *IT Standards, Guidelines, and Tools and Techniques for Audit and Assurance and Control Professionals,* ISACA.

2.22 When auditors cite compliance with both GAGAS and another set of standards, such as those listed in paragraphs 2.20 and 2.21, auditors should refer to paragraph 2.24 for the requirements for citing compliance with GAGAS. In addition to citing GAGAS, auditors may also cite the use of other standards in their reports when they have also met the requirements for citing compliance with the other standards.[27] Auditors should refer to the other set of standards for the basis for citing compliance with those standards.

Stating Compliance with GAGAS in the Auditors' Report

2.23 When auditors are required to perform an audit in accordance with GAGAS or are representing to others that they did so, they should cite compliance with GAGAS in the auditors' report as set forth in paragraphs 2.24 through 2.25.

---

[27]See paragraphs 4.18, 5.19, 5.51, and 5.61 for additional requirements for citing compliance with standards of the AICPA.

2.24 Auditors should include one of the following types of GAGAS compliance statements in reports on GAGAS audits, as appropriate.[28]

a. Unmodified GAGAS compliance statement: Stating that the auditor performed the audit in accordance with GAGAS. Auditors should include an unmodified GAGAS compliance statement in the auditors' report when they have (1) followed unconditional and applicable presumptively mandatory GAGAS requirements, or (2) have followed unconditional requirements, and documented justification for any departures from applicable presumptively mandatory requirements and have achieved the objectives of those requirements through other means.

b. Modified GAGAS compliance statement: Stating either that (1) the auditor performed the audit in accordance with GAGAS, except for specific applicable requirements that were not followed, or (2) because of the significance of the departure(s) from the requirements, the auditor was unable to and did not perform the audit in accordance with GAGAS. Situations when auditors use modified compliance statements also include scope limitations, such as restrictions on access to records, government officials, or other individuals needed to conduct the audit. When auditors use a modified GAGAS statement, they should disclose in the report the applicable requirement(s) not followed, the reasons for not following the requirement(s), and how not following the requirement(s) affected, or could have affected, the audit and the assurance provided.

---

[28]See paragraph A2.06 for additional discussion of GAGAS compliance statements.

2.25 When auditors do not comply with applicable requirement(s), they should (1) assess the significance of the noncompliance to the audit objectives, (2) document the assessment, along with their reasons for not following the requirement(s), and (3) determine the type of GAGAS compliance statement. The auditors' determination is a matter of professional judgment, which is affected by the significance of the requirement(s) not followed in relation to the audit objectives.

Chapter 3

General Standards

Introduction

3.01 This chapter establishes general standards and provides guidance for performing financial audits, attestation engagements, and performance audits under generally accepted government auditing standards (GAGAS). These general standards, along with the overarching ethical principles presented in chapter 1, establish a foundation for the credibility of auditors' work. These general standards emphasize the importance of the independence of the audit organization and its individual auditors; the exercise of professional judgment in the performance of work and the preparation of related reports; the competence of staff; and quality control and assurance.

Independence

3.02 In all matters relating to the audit work, the audit organization and the individual auditor, whether government or public, must be independent.

3.03 Independence comprises:

a. Independence of Mind
The state of mind that permits the performance of an audit without being affected by influences that compromise professional judgment, thereby allowing an individual to act with integrity and exercise objectivity and professional skepticism.

b. Independence in Appearance
The absence of circumstances that would cause a reasonable and informed third party, having knowledge of the relevant information, to reasonably conclude that the integrity, objectivity, or professional skepticism of an audit organization or member of the audit team had been compromised.

3.04 Auditors and audit organizations maintain independence so that their opinions, findings, conclusions, judgments, and recommendations will be impartial and viewed as impartial by reasonable and informed third parties. Auditors should avoid situations that could lead reasonable and informed third parties to conclude that the auditors are not independent and thus are not capable of exercising objective and impartial judgment on all issues associated with conducting the audit and reporting on the work.

3.05 Except under the limited circumstances discussed in paragraphs 3.47 and 3.48, auditors should be independent from an audited entity during:

a. any period of time that falls within the period covered by the financial statements or subject matter of the audit, and

b. the period of the professional engagement, which begins when the auditors either sign an initial engagement letter or other agreement to perform an audit or begin to perform an audit, whichever is earlier. The period lasts for the entire duration of the professional relationship (which, for recurring audits, could cover many periods) and ends with the formal or informal notification, either by the auditors or the audited entity, of the termination of the professional relationship or by the issuance of a report, whichever is later. Accordingly, the period of professional engagement does not necessarily end with the issuance of a report and recommence with the beginning of the following year's audit or a subsequent audit with a similar objective.

3.06 GAGAS's practical consideration of independence consists of four interrelated sections, providing:

a. a conceptual framework for making independence determinations based on facts and circumstances that are often unique to specific environments;

b. requirements for and guidance on independence for audit organizations that are structurally located within the entities they audit;

c. requirements for and guidance on independence for auditors performing nonaudit services, including indication of specific nonaudit services that always impair independence and others that would not normally impair independence; and

d. requirements for and guidance on documentation necessary to support adequate consideration of auditor independence.

GAGAS Conceptual Framework Approach to Independence	**3.07** Many different circumstances, or combinations of circumstances, are relevant in evaluating threats to independence. Therefore, GAGAS establishes a conceptual framework that auditors use to identify, evaluate, and apply safeguards to address threats to independence.[29] The conceptual framework assists auditors in maintaining both independence of mind and independence in appearance. It can be applied to many variations in circumstances that create threats to independence and allows auditors to address threats to independence that result from activities that are not specifically prohibited by GAGAS.

3.08 Auditors should apply the conceptual framework at the audit organization, audit, and individual auditor levels to:

a. identify threats to independence;

---

[29]See Appendix II for a flowchart to assist in the application of the conceptual framework for independence.

b. evaluate the significance of the threats identified, both individually and in the aggregate; and

c. apply safeguards as necessary to eliminate the threats or reduce them to an acceptable level.

3.09 If no safeguards are available to eliminate an unacceptable threat or reduce it to an acceptable level, independence would be considered impaired.

3.10 The use of the term "audit organization" in GAGAS is described in paragraph 1.07. For consideration of auditor independence, offices or units of an audit organization, or related or affiliated entities under common control, are not differentiated from one another. Consequently, for the purposes of independence evaluation using the conceptual framework, an audit organization that includes multiple offices or units, or includes multiple entities related or affiliated through common control, is considered to be one audit organization. Common ownership may also affect independence in appearance regardless of the level of control.

3.11 The GAGAS section on nonaudit services in paragraphs 3.33 through 3.58 provides requirements and guidance on evaluating threats to independence related to nonaudit services provided by auditors to audited entities. That section also enumerates specific nonaudit services that always impair auditor independence with respect to audited entities and that auditors are prohibited from providing to audited entities.

3.12 The following sections discuss threats to independence, safeguards or controls to eliminate or reduce threats, and application of the conceptual framework for independence.

Threats

3.13 Threats to independence are circumstances that could impair independence. Whether independence is impaired depends on the nature of the threat, whether the threat is of such significance that it would compromise an auditor's professional judgment or create the appearance that the auditor's professional judgment may be compromised, and on the specific safeguards applied to eliminate the threat or reduce it to an acceptable level. Threats are conditions to be evaluated using the conceptual framework. Threats do not necessarily impair independence.

3.14 Threats to independence may be created by a wide range of relationships and circumstances. Auditors should evaluate the following broad categories of threats to independence when threats are being identified and evaluated:[30]

a. Self-interest threat - the threat that a financial or other interest will inappropriately influence an auditor's judgment or behavior;

b. Self-review threat - the threat that an auditor or audit organization that has provided nonaudit services will not appropriately evaluate the results of previous judgments made or services performed as part of the nonaudit services when forming a judgment significant to an audit;

c. Bias threat - the threat that an auditor will, as a result of political, ideological, social, or other convictions, take a position that is not objective;

d. Familiarity threat - the threat that aspects of a relationship with management or personnel of an

---

[30]See A3.02 through A3.09 for further discussion and examples of threats.

audited entity, such as a close or long relationship, or that of an immediate or close family member, will lead an auditor to take a position that is not objective;

e. Undue influence threat - the threat that external influences or pressures will impact an auditor's ability to make independent and objective judgments;

f. Management participation threat - the threat that results from an auditor's taking on the role of management or otherwise performing management functions on behalf of the entity undergoing an audit; and

g. Structural threat - the threat that an audit organization's placement within a government entity, in combination with the structure of the government entity being audited, will impact the audit organization's ability to perform work and report results objectively.

3.15 Circumstances that result in a threat to independence in one of the above categories may result in other threats as well. For example, a circumstance resulting in a structural threat to independence may also expose auditors to undue influence and management participation threats.

Safeguards

3.16 Safeguards are controls designed to eliminate or reduce to an acceptable level threats to independence. Under the conceptual framework, the auditor applies safeguards that address the specific facts and circumstances under which threats to independence exist. In some cases, multiple safeguards may be necessary to address a threat. The list of safeguards in this section provides examples that may be effective under certain circumstances. The list cannot provide safeguards for all circumstances. It may, however, provide a starting point for auditors who have identified threats to independence and are considering what safeguards could eliminate those threats or reduce them to an acceptable level.

3.17 Examples of safeguards include:

a. consulting an independent third party, such as a professional organization, a professional regulatory body, or another auditor;

b. involving another audit organization to perform or reperform part of the audit;

c. having a professional staff member who was not a member of the audit team review the work performed; and

d. removing an individual from an audit team when that individual's financial or other interests or relationships pose a threat to independence.

3.18 Depending on the nature of the audit, an auditor may also be able to place limited reliance on safeguards that the entity has implemented. It is not possible to rely solely on such safeguards to eliminate threats or reduce them to an acceptable level.

3.19 Examples of safeguards within the entity's systems and procedures include:

a. an entity requirement that persons other than management ratify or approve the appointment of an audit organization to perform an audit;

b. internal procedures at the entity that ensure objective choices in commissioning nonaudit services; and

c. a governance structure at the entity that provides appropriate oversight and communications regarding the audit organization's services.

Application of the Conceptual Framework

3.20 Auditors should evaluate threats to independence using the conceptual framework when the facts and circumstances under which the auditors perform their work may create or augment threats to independence. Auditors should evaluate threats both individually and in the aggregate because threats can have a cumulative effect on an auditor's independence.

3.21 Facts and circumstances that create threats to independence can result from events such as the start of a new audit; assignment of new staff to an ongoing audit; and acceptance of a nonaudit service at an audited entity. Many other events can result in threats to independence. Auditors use professional judgment to determine whether the facts and circumstances created by an event warrant use of the conceptual framework. Whenever relevant new information about a threat to independence comes to the attention of the auditor during the audit, the auditor should evaluate the significance of the threat in accordance with the conceptual framework.

3.22 Auditors should determine whether identified threats to independence are at an acceptable level or have been eliminated or reduced to an acceptable level. A threat to independence is not acceptable if it either (a) could impact the auditor's ability to perform an audit without being affected by influences that compromise professional judgment or (b) could expose the auditor or audit organization to circumstances that would cause a reasonable and informed third party to conclude that the integrity, objectivity, or professional skepticism of the audit organization, or a member of the audit team, had been compromised.

3.23 When an auditor identifies threats to independence and, based on an evaluation of those threats, determines that they are not at an acceptable level, the auditor should determine whether appropriate safeguards are available and can be applied to eliminate the threats or reduce them to an acceptable level. The auditor should exercise professional judgment in making that determination, and should take into account whether both independence of mind and independence in appearance are maintained. The auditor should evaluate both qualitative and quantitative factors when determining the significance of a threat.

3.24 In cases where threats to independence are not at an acceptable level, thereby requiring the application of safeguards, the auditors should document the threats identified and the safeguards applied to eliminate the threats or reduce them to an acceptable level.

3.25 Certain conditions may lead to threats that are so significant that they cannot be eliminated or reduced to an acceptable level through the application of safeguards, resulting in impaired independence. Under such conditions, auditors should decline to perform a prospective audit or terminate an audit in progress.[31]

3.26 If a threat to independence is initially identified after the auditors' report is issued, the auditor should evaluate the threat's impact on the audit and on GAGAS compliance. If the auditors determine that the newly identified threat had an impact on the audit that would have resulted in the auditors' report being different from the report issued had the auditors been aware of it, they should communicate in the same manner as that used to originally distribute the report to those charged with governance, the appropriate officials of the audited entity, the appropriate officials of the

---

[31]See paragraph 3.44 for a discussion of conditions under which an auditor may be required by law or regulation to perform both an audit and a nonaudit service and cannot decline to perform or terminate the service. See the discussion of nonaudit services beginning in paragraph 3.45 for consideration of threats related to nonaudit services that cannot be eliminated or reduced to an appropriate level.

organizations requiring or arranging for the audits, and other known users, so that they do not continue to rely on findings or conclusions that were impacted by the threat to independence. If the report was previously posted to the auditors' publicly accessible website, the auditors should remove the report and post a public notification that the report was removed. The auditors should then determine whether to conduct additional audit work necessary to reissue the report, including any revised findings or conclusions or repost the original report if the additional audit work does not result in a change in findings or conclusions.

Government Auditors and Audit Organization Structure

3.27 The ability of audit organizations in government entities to perform work and report the results objectively can be affected by placement within government and the structure of the government entity being audited. The independence standard applies to auditors in government entities whether they report to third parties externally (external auditors), to senior management within the audited entity (internal auditors), or to both.

External Auditor Independence

3.28 Audit organizations that are structurally located within government entities are often subject to constitutional or statutory safeguards that mitigate the effects of structural threats to independence. For external audit organizations, such safeguards may include governmental structures under which a government audit organization is:

a. at a level of government other than the one of which the audited entity is part (federal, state, or local); for example, federal auditors auditing a state government program; or

b. placed within a different branch of government from that of the audited entity; for example, legislative auditors auditing an executive branch program.

3.29 Safeguards other than those described above may mitigate threats resulting from governmental structures. For external auditors or auditors who report both externally and internally, structural threats may be mitigated if the head of an audit organization meets any of the following criteria in accordance with constitutional or statutory requirements:

a. directly elected by voters of the jurisdiction being audited;

b. elected or appointed by a legislative body, subject to removal by a legislative body, and reports the results of audits to and is accountable to a legislative body;

c. appointed by someone other than a legislative body, so long as the appointment is confirmed by a legislative body and removal from the position is subject to oversight or approval by a legislative body, and reports the results of audits to and is accountable to a legislative body; or

d. appointed by, accountable to, reports to, and can only be removed by a statutorily created governing body, the majority of whose members are independently elected or appointed and are outside the organization being audited.

3.30 In addition to the criteria in paragraphs 3.28 and 3.29, GAGAS recognizes that there may be other organizational structures under which external audit organizations in government entities could be considered to be independent. If appropriately designed and implemented, these structures provide safeguards that prevent the audited entity from interfering with the audit organization's ability to perform the work and report the results impartially. For an external audit organization or one that reports both externally and internally to be considered independent under a structure different from the ones listed in paragraphs 3.28 and 3.29, the audit organization should have all of the following safeguards. In such situations, the audit organization should document how each of the following safeguards was satisfied and provide the documentation to those performing quality control monitoring and to the external peer reviewers to determine whether all the necessary safeguards are in place. The following safeguards may also be used to augment those listed in paragraphs 3.28 and 3.29:

a. statutory protections that prevent the audited entity from abolishing the audit organization;

b. statutory protections that require that if the head of the audit organization is removed from office, the head of the agency reports this fact and the reasons for the removal to the legislative body;

c. statutory protections that prevent the audited entity from interfering with the initiation, scope, timing, and completion of any audit;

d. statutory protections that prevent the audited entity from interfering with audit reporting, including the findings and conclusions or the manner, means, or timing of the audit organization's reports;

e. statutory protections that require the audit organization to report to a legislative body or other independent governing body on a recurring basis;

f. statutory protections that give the audit organization sole authority over the selection, retention, advancement, and dismissal of its staff; and

g. statutory access to records and documents related to the agency, program, or function being audited and access to government officials or other individuals as needed to conduct the audit.

Internal Auditor Independence

3.31 Certain entities employ auditors to work for entity management. These auditors may be subject to administrative direction from persons involved in the entity management process. Such audit organizations are internal audit functions and are encouraged to use the Institute of Internal Auditors (IIA) *International Standards for the Professional Practice of Internal Auditing* in conjunction with GAGAS. In accordance with GAGAS, internal auditors who work under the direction of the audited entity's management are considered independent for the purposes of reporting internally if the head of the audit organization meets all of the following criteria:

a. is accountable to the head or deputy head of the government entity or to those charged with governance;

b. reports the audit results both to the head or deputy head of the government entity and to those charged with governance;

c. is located organizationally outside the staff or line-management function of the unit under audit;

d. has access to those charged with governance; and

e. is sufficiently removed from political pressures to conduct audits and report findings, opinions, and conclusions objectively without fear of political reprisal.

3.32 When internal audit organizations perform audits of external parties such as auditing contractors or outside party agreements, and no impairments to independence exist, the audit organization can be

considered independent as an external audit
organization of those external parties.

Provision of Nonaudit Services to Audited Entities

3.33 Auditors have traditionally provided a range of nonaudit services that are consistent with their skills and expertise to entities at which they perform audits. Providing such nonaudit services may create threats to an auditor's independence.

Requirements for Performing Nonaudit Services

3.34 Before an auditor agrees to provide a nonaudit service to an audited entity, the auditor should determine whether providing such a service would create a threat to independence, either by itself or in aggregate with other nonaudit services provided, with respect to any GAGAS audit it performs. A critical component of this determination is consideration of management's ability to effectively oversee the nonaudit service to be performed. The auditor should determine that the audited entity has designated an individual who possesses suitable skill, knowledge, or experience, and that the individual understands the services to be performed sufficiently to oversee them. The individual is not required to possess the expertise to perform or reperform the services. The auditor should document consideration of management's ability to effectively oversee nonaudit services to be performed.

3.35 If an auditor were to assume management responsibilities for an audited entity, the management participation threats created would be so significant that no safeguards could reduce them to an acceptable level. Management responsibilities involve leading and directing an entity, including making decisions regarding the acquisition, deployment and control of human, financial, physical, and intangible resources.

3.36 Whether an activity is a management responsibility depends on the facts and circumstances and auditors exercise professional judgment in identifying these activities. Examples of activities that are considered management responsibilities and would therefore impair independence if performed for an audited entity include:

a. setting policies and strategic direction for the audited entity;

b. directing and accepting responsibility for the actions of the audited entity's employees in the performance of their routine, recurring activities;

c. having custody of an audited entity's assets;

d. reporting to those charged with governance on behalf of management;

e. deciding which of the auditor's or outside third party's recommendations to implement;

f. accepting responsibility for the management of an audited entity's project;

g. accepting responsibility for designing, implementing, or maintaining internal control;

h. providing services that are intended to be used as management's primary basis for making decisions that are significant to the subject matter of the audit;

i. developing an audited entity's performance measurement system when that system is material or significant to the subject matter of the audit; and

j. serving as a voting member of an audited entity's management committee or board of directors.

3.37 Auditors performing nonaudit services for entities for which they perform audits should obtain assurance that audited entity management performs the following functions in connection with the nonaudit services:

a. assumes all management responsibilities;

b. oversees the services, by designating an individual, preferably within senior management, who possess suitable skill, knowledge, or experience;[32]

c. evaluates the adequacy and results of the services performed; and

d. accepts responsibility for the results of the services.

3.38 In cases where the audited entity is unable or unwilling to assume these responsibilities (for example, the audited entity does not have an individual with suitable skill, knowledge, or experience to oversee the nonaudit services provided, or is unwilling to perform such functions due to lack of time or desire), the auditor's provision of these services would impair independence.

3.39 In connection with nonaudit services, auditors should establish and document their understanding with the audited entity's management or those charged with governance, as appropriate, regarding the following:

a. objectives of the nonaudit service;

b. services to be performed;

c. audited entity's acceptance of its responsibilities;

---

[32]See paragraph 3.34 for additional discussion of management's ability to effectively oversee the nonaudit service.

d. the auditor's responsibilities; and

e. any limitations of the nonaudit service.

3.40 Routine activities performed by auditors that relate directly to the performance of an audit, such as providing advice and responding to questions as part of an audit, are not considered nonaudit services under GAGAS. Such routine activities generally involve providing advice or assistance to the entity on an informal basis as part of an audit. Routine activities typically are insignificant in terms of time incurred or resources expended and generally do not result in a specific project or engagement or in the auditors producing a formal report or other formal work product. However, activities such as financial statement preparation, cash to accrual conversions, and reconciliations are considered nonaudit services under GAGAS, not routine activities related to the performance of an audit, and are evaluated using the conceptual framework as discussed in paragraph 3.46.

3.41 Routine activities directly related to an audit include the following:

a. providing advice to the audited entity on an accounting matter as an ancillary part of the overall financial audit;

b. researching and responding to the audited entity's technical questions on relevant tax laws as an ancillary part of providing tax services;

c. providing advice to the audited entity on routine business matters;

d. educating the audited entity on matters within the technical expertise of the auditors; and

e. providing information to the audited entity that is readily available to the auditors, such as best practices and benchmarking studies.

3.42 An auditor who previously performed nonaudit services for an entity that is a prospective subject of an audit should evaluate the impact of those nonaudit services on independence before accepting an audit. If the nonaudit services were performed in the period to be covered by the audit, the auditor should (1) determine if the nonaudit service is expressly prohibited by GAGAS and, if not, (2) determine whether a threat to independence exists and address any threats noted in accordance with the conceptual framework.

3.43 Nonaudit services provided by auditors can impact independence of mind and in appearance in periods subsequent to the period in which the nonaudit service was provided. For example, if auditors have designed and implemented an accounting and financial reporting system that is expected to be in place for many years, a threat to independence in appearance for future financial audits or attestation engagements performed by those auditors may exist in subsequent periods. For recurring audits, having another independent audit organization perform an audit of the areas affected by the nonaudit service may provide a safeguard that allows the audit organization that provided the nonaudit service to mitigate the threat to its independence. Auditors use professional judgment to determine whether the safeguards adequately mitigate the threats.

3.44 An auditor in a government entity may be required to perform a nonaudit service that could impair the auditor's independence with respect to a required audit. If the auditor cannot, as a consequence of constitutional or statutory requirements over which the auditor has no control, implement safeguards to reduce the resulting

threat to an acceptable level, or decline to perform or
terminate a nonaudit service that is incompatible with
audit responsibilities, the auditor should disclose the
nature of the threat that could not be eliminated or
reduced to an acceptable level and modify the GAGAS
compliance statement accordingly.[33]

Consideration of Specific Nonaudit Services

3.45 By their nature, certain nonaudit services directly
support the entity's operations and impair auditors'
ability to maintain independence in mind and
appearance. The nonaudit services discussed below
are among those frequently requested of auditors
working in a government environment. Some aspects of
these services will impair an auditor's ability to perform
audits for the entities for which the services are
provided. The specific services indicated are not the
only nonaudit services that would impair an auditor's
independence.

3.46 Auditors may be able to provide nonaudit services
in the broad areas indicated in paragraphs 3.49 through
3.58 without impairing independence if (1) the nonaudit
services are not expressly prohibited, (2) the auditor
has determined that the requirements for performing
nonaudit services in paragraphs 3.34 through 3.44 have
been met, and (3) any significant threats to
independence have been eliminated or reduced to an
acceptable level through the application of safeguards.
Auditors should use the conceptual framework to
evaluate independence given the facts and
circumstances of individual services not specifically
prohibited in this section.

3.47 For performance audits and agreed-upon
procedures engagements, nonaudit services that are

---

[33]See paragraphs 2.24 and 2.25 for the discussion of modifications to
the GAGAS compliance statement.

otherwise prohibited by GAGAS may be provided when such services do not relate to the specific subject matter of the engagement.

3.48 For financial statement audits and examination or review engagements, a nonaudit service performed during the period covered by the financial statements may not impair an auditor's independence with respect to those financial statements provided that the following conditions exist:

a. the nonaudit service was provided prior to the period of professional engagement;

b. the nonaudit service related only to periods prior to the period covered by the financial statements; and

c. the financial statements for the period to which the nonaudit service did relate were audited by another auditor (or in the case of an examination or review engagement, examined, reviewed, or audited by another auditor as appropriate).

Management Responsibilities

3.49 If performed on behalf of an audited entity by the entity's auditor, management responsibilities such as those listed in paragraph 3.36 would create management participation threats so significant that no safeguards could reduce them to an acceptable level. Consequently the auditor's independence would be impaired with respect to that entity.

Preparing Accounting Records and Financial Statements

3.50 Some services involving preparation of accounting records always impair an auditor's independence with respect to an audited entity. These services include:

a. determining or changing journal entries, account codes or classifications for transactions, or other accounting records for the entity without obtaining management's approval;

b. authorizing or approving the entity's transactions; and

c. preparing or making changes to source documents without management approval. Source documents include those providing evidence that transactions have occurred (for example, purchase orders, payroll time records, customer orders, and contracts). Such records also include an audited entity's general ledger and subsidiary records or equivalent.

3.51 Management is responsible for the preparation and fair presentation of the financial statements in accordance with the applicable financial reporting framework, even if the auditor assisted in drafting those financial statements. Consequently, an auditor's acceptance of responsibility for the preparation and fair presentation of financial statements that the auditor will subsequently audit would impair the auditor's independence.

3.52 Services related to preparing accounting records and financial statements that an auditor may be able to provide to an audited entity if the conditions in paragraph 3.46 are met include:

a. recording transactions for which management has determined or approved the appropriate account classification, or posting coded transactions to an audited entity's general ledger;

b. preparing financial statements based on information in the trial balance;

c. posting entries that have been approved by an audited entity's management to the entity's trial balance;

d. preparing account reconciliations that identify reconciling items for the audited entity management's evaluation; and

e. proposing standard, adjusting, or correcting journal entries or other changes affecting the financial statements to an audited entity's management provided management reviews and accepts the entries and the auditor is satisfied that management understands the nature of the proposed entries and the impact the entries have on the financial statements.

Internal Audit Assistance Services Provided by External Auditors

3.53 Internal audit assistance services involve assisting an entity in the performance of its internal audit activities. Certain internal audit assistance activities always impair an external auditor's independence with respect to an audited entity. These activities include:

a. setting internal audit policies or the strategic direction of internal audit activities;

b. performing procedures that form part of the internal control, such as reviewing and approving changes to employee data access privileges; and

c. determining the scope of the internal audit function and resulting work.

Internal Control Monitoring as a Nonaudit Service

3.54 Accepting responsibility for designing, implementing or maintaining internal control includes accepting responsibility for designing, implementing, or maintaining monitoring procedures.[34] Monitoring involves the use of either ongoing monitoring procedures or separate evaluations to gather and analyze persuasive information supporting conclusions about the effectiveness of the internal control system.

---

[34]See A.03 and A.04 for a discussion of internal control.

Ongoing monitoring procedures performed on behalf of management are built into the routine, recurring operating activities of an organization. Therefore, the management participation threat created if an auditor performs or supervises ongoing monitoring procedures is so significant that no safeguards could reduce the threat to an acceptable level.

3.55 Separate evaluations are sometimes performed as nonaudit services by individuals who are not directly involved in the operation of the controls being monitored. As such, it is possible for an auditor to provide an objective analysis of control effectiveness by performing separate evaluations without creating a management participation threat that would impair independence. However, in all such cases, the significance of the threat created by performing separate evaluations should be evaluated and safeguards applied when necessary to eliminate the threat or reduce it to an acceptable level. Auditors should assess the frequency of the separate evaluations as well as the scope or extent of the controls (in relation to the scope of the audit performed) being tested when evaluating the significance of the threat. An evaluation prepared as a nonaudit service is not a substitute for audit procedures in a GAGAS audit.

Information Technology Systems Services

3.56 Services related to information technology (IT) systems include the design or implementation of hardware or software systems. The systems may aggregate source data, form part of the internal control over the subject matter of the audit, or generate information that affects the subject matter of the audit. IT services that would impair independence if provided by an audit organization to an audited entity include:

a. designing or developing a financial or other IT system that will play a significant role in the management of an area of operations that is or will be the subject matter of an audit;

b. providing services that entail making other than insignificant modifications to the source code underlying such a system; and

c. operating or supervising the operation of such a system.

Valuation Services

3.57 A valuation comprises the making of assumptions with regard to future developments, the application of appropriate methodologies and techniques, and the combination of both to compute a certain value, or range of values, for an asset, a liability, or an entity as a whole. If an audit organization provides valuation services to an audited entity and the valuations would have a material effect, separately or in the aggregate, on the financial statements or other information on which it is reporting, and the valuation involves a significant degree of subjectivity, the audit organization's independence would be impaired.

Other Nonaudit Services

3.58 Provision of certain other nonaudit services always impairs an external auditor's independence with respect to an audited entity. These activities include:

a. Non tax disbursement – prohibited nonaudit services

(1) Accepting responsibility to authorize payment of audited entity funds, electronically or otherwise.

(2) Accepting responsibility for signing or cosigning audited entity checks, even if only in emergency situations.

(3) Maintaining an audited entity's bank account or otherwise having custody of an audited entity's funds or making credit or banking decisions for the audited entity.

(4) Approving vendor invoices for payment.

b. Benefit plan administration – prohibited nonaudit services

(1) Making policy decisions on behalf of audited entity management.

(2) When dealing with plan participants, interpreting the plan document on behalf of management without first obtaining management's concurrence.

(3) Making disbursements on behalf of the plan.

(4) Having custody of a plan's assets.

(5) Serving a plan as a fiduciary as defined by the Employee Retirement Income Security Act (ERISA).

c. Investment—advisory or management—prohibited nonaudit services

(1) Making investment decisions on behalf of audited entity management or otherwise having discretionary authority over an audited entity's investments.

(2) Executing a transaction to buy or sell an audited entity's investment.

(3) Having custody of an audited entity's assets, such as taking temporary possession of securities purchased by an audited entity.

d. Corporate finance—consulting or advisory – prohibited nonaudit services

(1) Committing the audited entity to the terms of a transaction or consummating a transaction on behalf of the audited entity.

(2) Acting as a promoter, underwriter, broker-dealer, or guarantor of audited entity securities, or distributor of private placement memoranda or offering documents.

(3) Maintaining custody of an audited entity's securities.

e. Executive or employee personnel matters – prohibited nonaudit services

(1) Committing the audited entity to employee compensation or benefit arrangements.

(2) Hiring or terminating audited entity employees.

f. Business risk consulting – prohibited nonaudit services

(1) Making or approving business risk decisions.

(2) Presenting business risk considerations to those charged with governance or others on behalf of management.

Documentation

3.59 Documentation of independence considerations provides evidence of the auditor's judgments in forming conclusions regarding compliance with independence requirements. GAGAS contains specific requirements for documentation related to independence which may be in addition to the documentation that auditors have previously maintained. While insufficient documentation of an auditor's compliance with the independence standard does not impair independence, appropriate documentation is required under the GAGAS quality control and assurance requirements.[35] The independence standard includes the following documentation requirements:

a. document threats to independence that require the application of safeguards, along with safeguards applied, in accordance with the conceptual framework for independence as required by paragraph 3.24;

b. document the safeguards required by paragraph 3.30 if an audit organization is structurally located within a government entity and is considered independent based on those safeguards;

c. document consideration of audited entity management's ability to effectively oversee a nonaudit service to be provided by the auditor as indicated in paragraph 3.34; and

d. document the auditor's understanding with an audited entity for which the auditor will perform a nonaudit service as indicated in paragraph 3.39.

Professional Judgment

3.60 Auditors must use professional judgment in planning and performing audits and in reporting the results.

3.61 Professional judgment includes exercising reasonable care and professional skepticism. Reasonable care includes acting diligently in accordance with applicable professional standards and ethical principles. Professional skepticism is an attitude that includes a questioning mind and a critical

---

[35]See paragraph 3.84 for additional discussion of documenting compliance with quality control policies and procedures and paragraph 3.88 for additional discussion of policies and procedures on independence, legal, and ethical requirements.

assessment of evidence. Professional skepticism includes a mindset in which auditors assume neither that management is dishonest nor of unquestioned honesty.

3.62 Using the auditors' professional knowledge, skills, and experience to diligently perform, in good faith and with integrity, the gathering of information and the objective evaluation of the sufficiency and appropriateness of evidence is a critical component of audits. Professional judgment and competence are interrelated because judgments made are dependent upon the auditors' competence.

3.63 Professional judgment represents the application of the collective knowledge, skills, and experiences of all the personnel involved with an audit, as well as the professional judgment of individual auditors. In addition to personnel directly involved in the audit, professional judgment may involve collaboration with other stakeholders, external specialists, and management in the audit organization.

3.64 Using professional judgment is important to auditors in carrying out all aspects of their professional responsibilities, including following the independence standards and related conceptual framework; maintaining objectivity and credibility; assigning competent staff to the audit; defining the scope of work; evaluating, documenting, and reporting the results of the work; and maintaining appropriate quality control over the audit process.

3.65 Using professional judgment is important to auditors in applying the conceptual framework to determine independence in a given situation. This includes the consideration of any threats to the auditor's independence and related safeguards which may mitigate the identified threats. Auditors use professional judgment in identifying and evaluating any threats to independence, including threats to the appearance of independence.[36]

3.66 Using professional judgment is important to auditors in determining the required level of understanding of the audit subject matter and related circumstances. This includes consideration about whether the audit team's collective experience, training, knowledge, skills, abilities, and overall understanding are sufficient to assess the risks that the subject matter of the audit may contain a significant inaccuracy or could be misinterpreted.

3.67 An auditor's consideration of the risk level of each audit, including the risk of arriving at improper conclusions, is also important. Within the context of audit risk, exercising professional judgment in determining the sufficiency and appropriateness of evidence to be used to support the findings and conclusions based on the audit objectives and any recommendations reported is an integral part of the audit process.

3.68 While this standard places responsibility on each auditor and audit organization to exercise professional judgment in planning and performing an audit, it does not imply unlimited responsibility, nor does it imply infallibility on the part of either the individual auditor or the audit organization. Absolute assurance is not attainable due to factors such as the nature of evidence and characteristics of fraud. Professional judgment does not mean eliminating all possible limitations or weaknesses associated with a specific audit, but rather identifying, assessing, mitigating, and explaining them.

---

[36]See paragraph 3.03 for a description of independence in appearance.

Competence

3.69 The staff assigned to perform the audit must collectively possess adequate professional competence needed to address the audit objectives and perform the work in accordance with GAGAS.

3.70 The audit organization's management should assess skill needs to consider whether its workforce has the essential skills that match those necessary to perform the particular audit. Accordingly, audit organizations should have a process for recruitment, hiring, continuous development, assignment, and evaluation of staff to maintain a competent workforce. The nature, extent, and formality of the process will depend on various factors such as the size of the audit organization, its structure, and its work.

3.71 Competence is derived from a blending of education and experience. Competencies are not necessarily measured by years of auditing experience because such a quantitative measurement may not accurately reflect the kinds of experiences gained by an auditor in any given time period. Maintaining competence through a commitment to learning and development throughout an auditor's professional life is an important element for auditors. Competence enables an auditor to make sound professional judgments.

Technical Knowledge

3.72 The staff assigned to conduct an audit in accordance with GAGAS should collectively possess the technical knowledge, skills, and experience necessary to be competent for the type of work being performed before beginning work on that audit. The staff assigned to a GAGAS audit should collectively possess

a. knowledge of GAGAS applicable to the type of work they are assigned and the education, skills, and experience to apply this knowledge to the work being performed;

b. general knowledge of the environment in which the audited entity operates and the subject matter;

c. skills to communicate clearly and effectively, both orally and in writing; and

d. skills appropriate for the work being performed; for example, skills in

(1) statistical or nonstatistical sampling if the work involves use of sampling;

(2) information technology if the work involves review of information systems;

(3) engineering if the work involves review of complex engineering data;

(4) specialized audit methodologies or analytical techniques, such as the use of complex survey instruments, actuarial-based estimates, or statistical analysis tests, as applicable; or

(5) specialized knowledge in subject matters, such as scientific, medical, environmental, educational, or any other specialized subject matter, if the work calls for such expertise.

Additional Qualifications for Financial Audits and Attestation Engagements

3.73 Auditors performing financial audits should be knowledgeable in U.S. generally accepted accounting principles (GAAP), or with the applicable financial reporting framework being used, and the American Institute of Certified Public Accountants' (AICPA)

Statements on Auditing Standards (SAS)[37]and they should be competent in applying these SASs to the audit work.

3.74 Similarly, auditors performing attestation engagements should be knowledgeable in the AICPA general attestation standard related to criteria, the AICPA attestation standards for field work and reporting, and the related Statements on Standards for Attestation Engagements (SSAE),[38] and they should be competent in applying these standards and SSAE to the attestation work.[39]

3.75 Auditors engaged to perform financial audits or attestation engagements should be licensed certified public accountants, persons working for a licensed certified public accounting firm or for a government auditing organization, or licensed accountants in states that have multi-class licensing systems that recognize licensed accountants other than certified public accountants.

Continuing Professional Education

3.76 Auditors performing work in accordance with GAGAS, including planning, directing, performing audit procedures, or reporting on an audit conducted in accordance with GAGAS, should maintain their professional competence through continuing professional education (CPE). Therefore, each auditor performing work in accordance with GAGAS should complete, every 2 years, at least 24 hours of CPE that

---

[37]See paragraph 2.08 and 4.01 for discussion of the AICPA standards incorporated into GAGAS for financial audits.

[38]See paragraphs 2.09 and 5.01 for discussion of the AICPA standards incorporated into GAGAS for attestation engagements.

[39]See paragraphs 2.19 through 2.22 for additional information on the relationship between GAGAS and other professional standards for financial audits and attestation engagements.

directly relates to government auditing, the government environment, or the specific or unique environment in which the audited entity operates. Auditors who are involved in any amount of planning, directing, or reporting on GAGAS audits and auditors who are not involved in those activities but charge 20 percent or more of their time annually to GAGAS audits should also obtain at least an additional 56 hours of CPE (for a total of 80 hours of CPE in every 2-year period) that enhances the auditor's professional proficiency to perform audits. Auditors required to take the total 80 hours of CPE should complete at least 20 hours of CPE in each year of the 2-year periods. Auditors hired or initially assigned to GAGAS audits after the beginning of an audit organization's 2-year CPE period should complete a prorated number of CPE hours.

3.77 CPE programs are structured educational activities with learning objectives designed to maintain or enhance participants' knowledge, skills, and abilities in areas applicable to performing audits. Determining what subjects are appropriate for individual auditors to satisfy both the 80-hour and the 24-hour requirements is a matter of professional judgment to be exercised by auditors in consultation with appropriate officials in their audit organizations. Among the considerations in exercising that judgment are the auditors' experience, the responsibilities they assume in performing GAGAS audits, and the operating environment of the audited entity.

3.78 Meeting CPE requirements is primarily the responsibility of individual auditors. The audit organization should have quality control procedures to help ensure that auditors meet the continuing education requirements, including documentation of the CPE completed. The Government Accountability Office (GAO) has developed guidance pertaining to CPE requirements to assist auditors and audit organizations in exercising professional judgment in complying with the CPE requirements.[40]

CPE Requirements for Specialists

3.79 The audit team should determine that external specialists assisting in performing a GAGAS audit are qualified and competent in their areas of specialization; however, external specialists are not required to meet the GAGAS CPE requirements.

3.80 The audit team should determine that internal specialists consulting on a GAGAS audit who are not involved in directing, performing audit procedures, or reporting on a GAGAS audit, are qualified and competent in their areas of specialization; however, these internal specialists are not required to meet the GAGAS CPE requirements.

3.81 The audit team should determine that internal specialists, who are performing work in accordance with GAGAS as part of the audit team, including directing, performing audit procedures, or reporting on a GAGAS audit, comply with GAGAS, including the CPE requirements.[41] The GAGAS CPE requirements become effective for internal specialists when an audit organization first assigns an internal specialist to an audit. Because internal specialists apply specialized knowledge in government audits, training in their areas of specialization qualify under the requirement for 24 hours of CPE that directly relates to government auditing, the government environment, or the specific or unique environment in which the audited entity operates.

---

[40]*Government Auditing Standards: Guidance on GAGAS Requirements for Continuing Professional Education*, GAO-05-568G (Washington, D.C.: April 2005), http://www.gao.gov/yellowbook.

[41]See paragraphs 3.76 through 3.81 for discussion of the CPE requirements.

Quality Control and Assurance

3.82 Each audit organization performing audits in accordance with GAGAS must:

a. establish and maintain a system of quality control that is designed to provide the audit organization with reasonable assurance that the organization and its personnel comply with professional standards and applicable legal and regulatory requirements,[42] and

b. have an external peer review performed by reviewers independent of the audit organization being reviewed at least once every 3 years.

System of Quality Control

3.83 An audit organization's system of quality control encompasses the audit organization's leadership, emphasis on performing high quality work, and the organization's policies and procedures designed to provide reasonable assurance of complying with professional standards and applicable legal and regulatory requirements. The nature, extent, and formality of an audit organization's quality control system will vary based on the audit organization's circumstances, such as the audit organization's size, number of offices and geographic dispersion, knowledge and experience of its personnel, nature and complexity of its audit work, and cost-benefit considerations.

3.84 Each audit organization should document its quality control policies and procedures and communicate those policies and procedures to its personnel. The audit organization should document compliance with its quality control policies and procedures and maintain such documentation for a

---

[42]See paragraph A3.10 for additional discussion of the system of quality control.

period of time sufficient to enable those performing monitoring procedures and peer reviews to evaluate the extent of the audit organization's compliance with its quality control policies and procedures. The form and content of such documentation are a matter of professional judgment and will vary based on the audit organization's circumstances.

3.85 An audit organization should establish policies and procedures in its system of quality control that collectively address

a. leadership responsibilities for quality within the audit organization,

b. independence, legal, and ethical requirements,

c. initiation, acceptance, and continuance of audits,

d. human resources,

e. audit performance, documentation, and reporting, and

f. monitoring of quality.

Leadership Responsibilities for Quality within the Audit Organization

3.86 Audit organizations should establish policies and procedures on leadership responsibilities for quality within the audit organization that include the designation of responsibility for quality of audits performed in accordance with GAGAS and communication of policies and procedures relating to quality. Appropriate policies and communications encourage a culture that recognizes that quality is essential in performing GAGAS audits and that leadership of the audit organization is ultimately responsible for the system of quality control.

3.87 The audit organization should establish policies and procedures designed to provide it with reasonable assurance that those assigned operational responsibility for the audit organization's system of quality control have sufficient and appropriate experience and ability, and the necessary authority, to assume that responsibility.

Independence, Legal, and Ethical Requirements

3.88 Audit organizations should establish policies and procedures on independence, legal, and ethical requirements that are designed to provide reasonable assurance that the audit organization and its personnel maintain independence and comply with applicable legal and ethical requirements.[43] Such policies and procedures assist the audit organization to

a. communicate its independence requirements to its staff, and

b. identify and evaluate circumstances and relationships that create threats to independence, and take appropriate action to eliminate those threats or reduce them to an acceptable level by applying safeguards, or, if considered appropriate, withdraw from the audit where withdrawal is not prohibited by law or regulation.

Initiation, Acceptance, and Continuance of Audits

3.89 Audit organizations should establish policies and procedures for the initiation, acceptance, and continuance of audits that are designed to provide reasonable assurance that the audit organization will undertake audits only if it can comply with professional standards, legal requirements, and ethical principles

---

[43]See paragraphs 3.02 through 3.59 for GAGAS independence requirements. See chapter 1 for GAGAS ethical principles.

and is acting within the legal mandate or authority of the audit organization.[44]

Human Resources

3.90 Audit organizations should establish policies and procedures for human resources that are designed to provide the audit organization with reasonable assurance that it has personnel with the capabilities and competence to perform its audits in accordance with professional standards and legal and regulatory requirements.[45]

Audit Performance, Documentation, and Reporting

3.91 Audit organizations should establish policies and procedures for audit performance, documentation, and reporting that are designed to provide the audit organization with reasonable assurance that audits are performed and reports are issued in accordance with professional standards and legal and regulatory requirements.[46]

3.92 When performing GAGAS audits, audit organizations should have policies and procedures for the safe custody and retention of audit documentation for a time sufficient to satisfy legal, regulatory, and administrative requirements for records retention. Whether audit documentation is in paper, electronic, or other media, the integrity, accessibility, and retrievability of the underlying information could be compromised if the documentation is altered, added to, or deleted without the auditors' knowledge, or if the documentation is lost or damaged. For audit documentation that is retained electronically, the audit organization should

---

[44]See paragraph A3.10a for discussion of initiation of audits by government audit organizations.

[45]See paragraphs 3.69 through 3.81 for requirements related to professional competence.

[46]For financial audits, chapters 2 through 4 apply; for attestation engagements, chapters 2, 3 and 5 apply; for performance audits, chapters 2, 3, 6, and 7 apply.

establish effective information systems controls concerning accessing and updating the audit documentation.

Monitoring of Quality

3.93 Audit organizations should establish policies and procedures for monitoring of quality in the audit organization.[47] Monitoring of quality is an ongoing, periodic assessment of work completed on audits designed to provide management of the audit organization with reasonable assurance that the policies and procedures related to the system of quality control are suitably designed and operating effectively in practice. The purpose of monitoring compliance with quality control policies and procedures is to provide an evaluation of whether the:

a. professional standards and legal and regulatory requirements have been followed,

b. quality control system has been appropriately designed, and

c. quality control policies and procedures are operating effectively and complied with in practice.

3.94 Monitoring procedures will vary based on the audit organization's facts and circumstances. The audit organization should perform monitoring procedures that enable it to assess compliance with applicable professional standards and quality control policies and procedures for GAGAS audits. Individuals performing monitoring should collectively have sufficient expertise and authority for this role.

3.95 The audit organization should analyze and summarize the results of its monitoring process at least

---

[47]See paragraph A3.10c for additional discussion of monitoring.

annually, with identification of any systemic or repetitive issues needing improvement, along with recommendations for corrective action. The audit organization should communicate to appropriate personnel any deficiencies noted during the monitoring process and make recommendations for appropriate remedial action.

External Peer Review

3.96 The audit organization should obtain an external peer review at least once every 3 years that is sufficient in scope to provide a reasonable basis for determining whether, for the period under review, the reviewed audit organization's system of quality control was suitably designed and whether the audit organization is complying with its quality control system in order to provide the audit organization with reasonable assurance of conforming with applicable professional standards.

3.97 The first peer review for an audit organization not already subject to a peer review requirement covers a review period ending no later than 3 years from the date an audit organization begins its first audit in accordance with GAGAS. The period under review generally covers 1 year, although peer review programs may choose a longer review period. Generally, the deadlines for peer review reports are established by the entity that administers the peer review program. Extensions of the deadlines for submitting the peer review report exceeding 3 months beyond the due date are granted by the entity that administers the peer review program and GAO.

3.98 The peer review team should include the following elements in the scope of the peer review:

a. review of the audit organization's quality control policies and procedures;

b. consideration of the adequacy and results of the audit organization's internal monitoring procedures;

c. review of selected auditors' reports and related documentation;

d. review of other documents necessary for assessing compliance with standards, for example, independence documentation, CPE records, and relevant human resource management files; and

e. interviews with a selection of the reviewed audit organization's professional staff at various levels to assess their understanding of and compliance with relevant quality control policies and procedures.

3.99 The peer review team should perform an assessment of peer review risk to help determine the number and types of audits to select for review.[48] Based on the risk assessment, the team should use one or a combination of the following approaches to select individual audits for review with greater emphasis on those audits with higher assessed levels of peer review risk: (1) select GAGAS audits that provide a reasonable cross-section of the GAGAS audits performed by the reviewed audit organization; or (2) select audits that provide a reasonable cross-section from all types of work subject to the reviewed audit organization's quality control system, including one or more audits performed in accordance with GAGAS. The second approach is generally applicable to audit organizations that perform only a small number of GAGAS audits in relation to other types of audits. In these cases, one or more GAGAS audits may represent more than what would be

---

[48]See paragraph A3.11 for examples of factors to consider in assessing peer review risk.

selected when looking at a cross-section of the audit organization's work as a whole.

3.100 The peer review team should prepare one or more written reports communicating the results of the peer review, including the following:

a. a description of the scope of the peer review, including any limitations;

b. an opinion on whether the system of quality control of the reviewed audit organization's audit practices was adequately designed and complied with during the period reviewed to provide the audit organization with reasonable assurance of conforming with applicable professional standards;

c. specification of the professional standards to which the reviewed audit organization is being held; and

d. reference to a separate written communication, if issued under the peer review program.

3.101 The peer review team uses professional judgment in deciding the type of peer review report. The following are the types of peer review reports.

a. Peer Review Rating of Pass: A conclusion that the audit organization's system of quality control has been suitably designed and complied with to provide the audit organization with reasonable assurance of performing and reporting in conformity with applicable professional standards in all material respects.

b. Peer Review Rating of Pass with Deficiencies: A conclusion that the audit organization's system of quality control has been suitably designed and complied with to provide the audit organization with reasonable assurance of performing and reporting in conformity with applicable professional standards in all material respects with the exception of a certain deficiency or deficiencies that are described in the report.

c. Peer Review Rating of Fail: A conclusion, based on the significant deficiencies that are described in the report, that the audit organization's system of quality control is not suitably designed to provide the audit organization with reasonable assurance of performing and reporting in conformity with applicable professional standards in all material respects, or the audit organization has not complied with its system of quality control to provide the audit organization with reasonable assurance of performing and reporting in conformity with applicable professional standards in all material respects.

3.102 When the scope of the review is limited by conditions that preclude the application of one or more peer review procedures considered necessary in the circumstances and the peer reviewer cannot accomplish the objectives of those procedures through alternative procedures, the types of reports described in paragraphs 3.101 a-c are modified by including statements in the report's scope paragraph, body and opinion paragraph. These statements describe the relationship of the excluded audit(s) or functional area(s) to the reviewed organization's full scope of practice and system of quality control and the effects of the exclusion on the scope and results of the review.

3.103 For any deficiencies or significant deficiencies included in the peer review report or other written communication, the peer review team should include, either in the peer review report or in a separate written communication, a detailed description of the findings, conclusions, and recommendations related to the deficiencies or significant deficiencies.

3.104 The peer review team should meet the following criteria:

a. The review team collectively has current knowledge of GAGAS and government auditing.

b. The organization conducting the peer review and individual review team members are independent (as defined in GAGAS)[49] of the audit organization being reviewed, its staff, and the audits selected for the peer review.

c. The review team collectively has sufficient knowledge of how to perform a peer review. Such knowledge may be obtained from on-the-job training, training courses, or a combination of both. Having personnel on the peer review team with prior experience on a peer review or internal inspection team is desirable.

3.105 An external audit organization[50] should make its most recent peer review report publicly available.[51] For example, an audit organization may satisfy this requirement by posting the peer review report on a publicly available web site or to a publicly available file designed for public transparency of peer review results. Alternatively, if neither of these options is available to the audit organization, then it should use the same transparency mechanism it uses to make other information public. The audit organization should provide the peer review report to others upon request. If a separate communication detailing findings, conclusions, and recommendations is issued, public

---

[49]See paragraphs 3.02 through 3.32 for discussion of independence.

[50]See paragraph 1.07b for the definition of "audit organizations" and paragraph 1.08 for discussion of external audit organizations.

[51]See paragraph A3.12 for additional discussion of peer review report transparency.

availability of that communication is not required.
Internal audit organizations that report internally to
management and those charged with governance
should provide a copy of the peer review report to those
charged with governance.

3.106 Information in peer review reports may be
relevant to decisions on procuring audits. Therefore,
audit organizations seeking to enter into a contract to
perform an audit in accordance with GAGAS should
provide the following to the party contracting for such
services when requested:

a. the audit organization's most recent peer review
report, and

b. any subsequent peer review reports received during
the period of the contract.

3.107 Auditors who are using another audit
organization's work should request a copy of the audit
organization's latest peer review report and any other
written communication issued, and the audit
organization should provide these documents when
requested.[52]

---

[52]See paragraphs 6.40 through 6.44 for additional discussion on using
the work of other auditors.

Chapter 4

Standards for Financial Audits

Introduction

4.01 This chapter contains requirements, guidance, and considerations for performing and reporting on financial audits conducted in accordance with generally accepted government auditing standards (GAGAS). GAGAS incorporates by reference the American Institute of Certified Public Accountants (AICPA) Statements on Auditing Standards (SAS), as discussed in paragraph 2.08.[53] All sections of the SASs are incorporated, including the introduction, objectives, definitions, requirements, and application and other explanatory material. Auditors performing financial audits in accordance with GAGAS should comply with the incorporated SASs and the additional requirements in this chapter. The requirements and guidance contained in chapters 1 through 3 also apply to financial audits performed in accordance with GAGAS.

Additional GAGAS Requirements for Performing Financial Audits

4.02 GAGAS establishes requirements for performing financial audits in addition to the requirements contained in the AICPA standards. Auditors should comply with these additional requirements, along with the incorporated SASs, when citing GAGAS in their reports. The additional requirements for performing financial audits relate to:

a. auditor communication;

b. previous audits and attestation engagements;

---

[53]See the AICPA *Codification of Statements on Auditing Standards* and paragraph 2.20 for additional discussion on the relationship between GAGAS and other professional standards. References to the AICPA *Codification of Statements on Auditing Standards* use an "AU-C" identifier to refer to the clarified SASs instead of an "AU" identifier. "AU-C" is a temporary identifier to avoid confusion with references to existing "AU" sections, which remain effective through 2013. The "AU-C" identifier will revert to "AU" in 2014 AICPA *Codification of Statements on Auditing Standards*, by which time the clarified SASs become fully effective for all engagements.

c. fraud, noncompliance with provisions of laws, regulations, contracts, and grant agreements, and abuse;

d. developing elements of a finding; and

e. audit documentation.[54]

Auditor Communication

4.03 In addition to the AICPA requirements for auditor communication,[55] when performing a GAGAS financial audit, auditors should communicate pertinent information that in the auditors' professional judgment needs to be communicated to individuals contracting for or requesting the audit, and to cognizant legislative committees when auditors perform the audit pursuant to a law or regulation, or they conduct the work for the legislative committee that has oversight of the audited entity. This requirement does not apply if the law or regulation requiring an audit of the financial statements does not specifically identify the entities to be audited, such as audits required by the Single Audit Act Amendments of 1996.

4.04 In those situations where there is not a single individual or group that both oversees the strategic direction of the audited entity and the fulfillment of its accountability obligations or in other situations where the identity of those charged with governance is not clearly evident, auditors should document the process followed and conclusions reached for identifying the appropriate individuals to receive the required auditor communications.

---

[54]See paragraphs 4.03 through 4.16 for additional discussion of paragraph 4.02 a-e.

[55]See AICPA AU-C Section 260, *The Auditor's Communication With Those Charged With Governance.*

Previous Audits and Attestation Engagements

4.05 When performing a GAGAS audit, auditors should evaluate whether the audited entity has taken appropriate corrective action to address findings and recommendations from previous engagements that could have a material effect on the financial statements or other financial data significant to the audit objectives. When planning the audit, auditors should ask management of the audited entity to identify previous audits, attestation engagements, and other studies that directly relate to the objectives of the audit, including whether related recommendations have been implemented. Auditors should use this information in assessing risk and determining the nature, timing, and extent of current audit work, including determining the extent to which testing the implementation of the corrective actions is applicable to the current audit objectives.

Fraud, Noncompliance with Provisions of Laws, Regulations, Contracts, and Grant Agreements, and Abuse

4.06 In addition to the AICPA requirements concerning fraud[56] and noncompliance with provisions of laws and regulations,[57] when performing a GAGAS financial audit, auditors should extend the AICPA requirements pertaining to the auditors' responsibilities for laws and regulations to also apply to consideration of compliance with provisions of contracts or grant agreements.

4.07 Abuse involves behavior that is deficient or improper when compared with behavior that a prudent person would consider reasonable and necessary business practice given the facts and circumstances. Abuse also includes misuse of authority or position for personal financial interests or those of an immediate or

---

[56]See AICPA AU-C Section 240, *Consideration of Fraud in a Financial Statement Audit.*

[57]See AICPA AU-C Section 250, *Consideration of Laws and Regulations in an Audit of Financial Statements.*

close family member or business associate.[58] Abuse does not necessarily involve fraud, or noncompliance with provisions of laws, regulations, contracts, or grant agreements.

4.08 Because the determination of abuse is subjective, auditors are not required to detect abuse in financial audits. However, as part of a GAGAS audit, if auditors become aware of abuse that could be quantitatively or qualitatively material to the financial statements or other financial data significant to the audit objectives, auditors should apply audit procedures specifically directed to ascertain the potential effect on the financial statements or other financial data significant to the audit objectives. After performing additional work, auditors may discover that the abuse represents potential fraud or noncompliance with provisions of laws, regulations, contracts, or grant agreements.

4.09 Avoiding interference with investigations or legal proceedings is important in pursuing indications of fraud, noncompliance with provisions of laws, regulations, contracts, or grant agreements, or abuse. Laws, regulations, or policies may require auditors to report indications of certain types of fraud, noncompliance with provisions of laws, regulations, contracts or grant agreements, or abuse to law enforcement or investigatory authorities before performing additional audit procedures. When investigations or legal proceedings are initiated or in process, auditors should evaluate the impact on the current audit. In some cases, it may be appropriate for the auditors to work with investigators or legal authorities, or withdraw from or defer further work on the audit engagement or a portion of the engagement to

---

[58]See paragraph A.08 for additional examples of abuse.

avoid interfering with an ongoing investigation or legal proceeding.

Developing Elements of a Finding

4.10 In a financial audit, findings may involve deficiencies in internal control; noncompliance with provisions of laws, regulations, contracts, or grant agreements; fraud; or abuse. As part of a GAGAS audit, when auditors identify findings, auditors should plan and perform procedures to develop the elements of the findings that are relevant and necessary to achieve the audit objectives. The elements of a finding are discussed in paragraphs 4.11 through 4.14 below.

4.11 Criteria: The laws, regulations, contracts, grant agreements, standards, measures, expected performance, defined business practices, and benchmarks against which performance is compared or evaluated. Criteria identify the required or desired state or expectation with respect to the program or operation. Criteria provide a context for evaluating evidence and understanding the findings.

4.12 Condition: Condition is a situation that exists. The condition is determined and documented during the audit.

4.13 Cause: The cause identifies the reason or explanation for the condition or the factor or factors responsible for the difference between the situation that exists (condition) and the required or desired state (criteria), which may also serve as a basis for recommendations for corrective actions. Common factors include poorly designed policies, procedures, or criteria; inconsistent, incomplete, or incorrect implementation; or factors beyond the control of program management. Auditors may assess whether the evidence provides a reasonable and convincing argument for why the stated cause is the key factor or factors contributing to the difference between the condition and the criteria.

4.14 Effect or potential effect: The effect is a clear, logical link to establish the impact or potential impact of the difference between the situation that exists (condition) and the required or desired state (criteria). The effect or potential effect identifies the outcomes or consequences of the condition. When the audit objectives include identifying the actual or potential consequences of a condition that varies (either positively or negatively) from the criteria identified in the audit, "effect" is a measure of those consequences. Effect or potential effect may be used to demonstrate the need for corrective action in response to identified problems or relevant risks.

Audit Documentation

4.15 In addition to the AICPA requirements for audit documentation,[59] auditors should comply with the following additional requirements when performing a GAGAS financial audit.[60]

a. Document supervisory review, before the report release date, of the evidence that supports the findings, conclusions, and recommendations contained in the auditors' report.

b. Document any departures from the GAGAS requirements and the impact on the audit and on the auditors' conclusions when the audit is not in compliance with applicable GAGAS requirements due to law, regulation, scope limitations, restrictions on access to records, or other issues impacting the audit.

---

[59]See AICPA AU-C Section 230, *Audit Documentation*.

[60]See paragraphs 4.04, 4.06, 4.26, and 4.45 for additional documentation requirements regarding financial audits.

This applies to departures from unconditional requirements and presumptively mandatory requirements when alternative procedures performed in the circumstances were not sufficient to achieve the objectives of the requirements.[61]

4.16 When performing GAGAS financial audits and subject to applicable provisions of laws and regulations, auditors should make appropriate individuals, as well as audit documentation, available upon request and in a timely manner to other auditors or reviewers. Underlying GAGAS audits is the premise that audit organizations in federal, state, and local governments and public accounting firms engaged to perform a financial audit in accordance with GAGAS cooperate in auditing programs of common interest so that auditors may use others' work and avoid duplication of efforts. The use of auditors' work by other auditors may be facilitated by contractual arrangements for GAGAS audits that provide for full and timely access to appropriate individuals, as well as audit documentation.

Additional GAGAS Requirements for Reporting on Financial Audits

4.17 In addition to the AICPA requirements for reporting,[62] auditors should comply with the following additional requirements when citing GAGAS in their reports. The additional requirements relate to

a. reporting auditors' compliance with GAGAS;

---

[61]See paragraphs 2.24 and 2.25 for additional requirements on citing compliance with GAGAS.

[62]See AICPA AU-C Sections 700 *Forming an Opinion and Reporting on Financial Statements;* 705 *Modifications to the Opinion in the Independent Auditor's Report,* and 706 *Emphasis-of-Matter Paragraphs and Other-Matter Paragraphs in the Independent Auditor's Report.*

b. reporting on internal control and compliance with provisions of laws, regulations, contracts, and grant agreements;

c. communicating deficiencies in internal control, fraud, noncompliance with provisions of laws, regulations, contracts, and grant agreements, and abuse;

d. reporting views of responsible officials;

e. reporting confidential or sensitive information; and

f. distributing reports.[63]

Reporting Auditors' Compliance with GAGAS

4.18 When auditors comply with all applicable GAGAS requirements for financial audits, they should include a statement in the auditors' report that they performed the audit in accordance with GAGAS.[64] Because GAGAS incorporates by reference the AICPA SASs,[65] GAGAS does not require auditors to cite compliance with the AICPA standards when citing compliance with GAGAS. Additionally, an entity receiving a GAGAS auditors' report may also request auditors to issue a financial audit report for purposes other than complying with requirements for a GAGAS audit. GAGAS does not prohibit auditors from issuing a separate report conforming only to AICPA or other standards.[66]

---

[63]See paragraphs 4.18 through 4.45 for additional discussion paragraph of 4.17 a-f.

[64]See paragraphs 2.24 and 2.25 for additional requirements on citing compliance with GAGAS.

[65]See paragraph 2.08 for a discussion of the AICPA SASs incorporated into GAGAS.

[66]See AICPA AU-C Section 700, *Forming an Opinion and Reporting on Financial Statements.*

Reporting on Internal Control and Compliance with Provisions of Laws, Regulations, Contracts, and Grant Agreements

4.19 When providing an opinion or a disclaimer on financial statements, auditors should also report on internal control over financial reporting[67] and on compliance with provisions of laws, regulations, contracts, or grant agreements that have a material effect on the financial statements.[68] Auditors report on internal control and compliance, regardless of whether or not they identify internal control deficiencies or instances of noncompliance.

4.20 Auditors should include either in the same or in separate report(s) a description of the scope of the auditors' testing of internal control over financial reporting and of compliance with provisions of laws, regulations, contracts, or grant agreements. Auditors should also state in the reports whether the tests they performed provided sufficient, appropriate evidence to support opinions on the effectiveness of internal control and on compliance with provisions of laws, regulations, contracts, or grant agreements.

4.21 The objective of the GAGAS requirement for reporting on internal control over financial reporting differs from the objective of an examination of internal control in accordance with the AICPA Statement on Standards for Attestation Engagements (SSAE), which is to express an opinion on the design or the design and operating effectiveness of an entity's internal control, as applicable. To form a basis for expressing such an opinion, the auditor would need to plan and perform the examination to provide a high level of assurance about whether the entity maintained, in all material respects, effective internal control over financial reporting as of a

---

[67]See paragraph A.05 for examples of deficiencies in internal control.

[68]See paragraph A.11 for additional discussion of laws, regulations, and provisions of contract and grant agreements.

point in time or for a specified period of time.[69] If auditors issue an opinion on internal control, the opinion would satisfy the GAGAS requirement for reporting on internal control.

4.22 If auditors report separately (including separate reports bound in the same document) on internal control over financial reporting and on compliance with provisions of laws, regulations, contracts, and grant agreements, they should state in the auditors' report on the financial statements that they are issuing those additional reports. They should include a reference to the separate reports and also state that the reports on internal control over financial reporting and on compliance with provisions of laws, regulations, contracts, and grant agreements are an integral part of a GAGAS audit in considering the audited entity's internal control over financial reporting and compliance.

Communicating Deficiencies in Internal Control, Fraud, Noncompliance with Provisions of Laws, Regulations, Contracts, and Grant Agreements, and Abuse

4.23 When performing GAGAS financial audits, auditors should communicate in the report on internal control over financial reporting and compliance, based upon the work performed, (1) significant deficiencies and material weaknesses in internal control; (2) instances of fraud and noncompliance with provisions of laws or regulations that have a material effect on the audit and any other instances that warrant the attention of those charged with governance; (3) noncompliance with provisions of contracts or grant agreements that has a material effect on the audit; and (4) abuse that has a material effect on the audit.

Deficiencies in Internal Control

4.24 The AICPA requirements to communicate in writing significant deficiencies and material weaknesses

---

[69]See AICPA AT Section 501, *An Examination of an Entity's Internal Control Over Financial Reporting That Is Integrated With an Audit of Its Financial Statements.*

identified during an audit[70] form the basis for reporting significant deficiencies and material weaknesses in the GAGAS report on internal control over financial reporting when deficiencies are identified during the audit.

Fraud, Noncompliance with Provisions of Laws, Regulations, Contracts, and Grant Agreements, and Abuse

4.25 When performing a GAGAS financial audit, and auditors conclude, based on sufficient, appropriate evidence, that any of the following either has occurred or is likely to have occurred, they should include in their report on internal control and compliance the relevant information about

a. fraud[71] and noncompliance with provisions of laws or regulations that have a material effect on the financial statements or other financial data significant to the audit objectives and any other instances that warrant the attention of those charged with governance;

b. noncompliance with provisions of contracts or grant agreements that has a material effect on the determination of financial statement amounts or other financial data significant to the audit objectives; or

c. abuse[72] that is material, either quantitatively or qualitatively.[73]

4.26 When auditors detect instances of noncompliance with provisions of contracts or grant agreements or abuse that have an effect on the financial statements or other financial data significant to the audit objectives

---

[70]See AICPA AU-C Section 265, *Communicating Internal Control Related Matters Identified in an Audit.*

[71]See paragraph A.10 for examples of indicators of fraud risk.

[72]See paragraph A.08 for examples of abuse.

[73]See paragraphs 4.07 and 4.08 for a discussion of abuse.

that are less than material but warrant the attention of those charged with governance, they should communicate those findings in writing to audited entity officials. When auditors detect any instances of fraud, noncompliance with provisions of laws, regulations, contracts or grant agreements, or abuse that do not warrant the attention of those charged with governance, the auditors' determination of whether and how to communicate such instances to audited entity officials is a matter of professional judgment.

4.27 When fraud, noncompliance with provisions of laws, regulations, contracts, or grant agreements, or abuse either have occurred or are likely to have occurred, auditors may consult with authorities or legal counsel about whether publicly reporting such information would compromise investigative or legal proceedings. Auditors may limit their public reporting to matters that would not compromise those proceedings, and for example, report only on information that is already a part of the public record.

Presenting Findings in the Auditors' Report

4.28 When performing a GAGAS financial audit and presenting findings such as deficiencies in internal control, fraud, noncompliance with provisions of laws, regulations, contracts, or grant agreements, or abuse, auditors should develop the elements of the findings to the extent necessary, including findings related to deficiencies from the previous year that have not been remediated. Clearly developed findings, as discussed in paragraphs 4.10 through 4.14, assist management or oversight officials of the audited entity in understanding the need for taking corrective action, and assist auditors in making recommendations for corrective action. If auditors sufficiently develop the elements of a finding, they may provide recommendations for corrective action.

4.29 Auditors should place their findings in perspective by describing the nature and extent of the issues being reported and the extent of the work performed that resulted in the finding. To give the reader a basis for judging the prevalence and consequences of these findings, auditors should, as appropriate, relate the instances identified to the population or the number of cases examined and quantify the results in terms of dollar value or other measures. If the results cannot be projected, auditors should limit their conclusions appropriately.

Reporting Findings Directly to Parties Outside the Audited Entity

4.30 Auditors should report known or likely fraud, noncompliance with provisions of laws, regulations, contracts, or grant agreements, or abuse directly to parties outside the audited entity in the following two circumstances.

a. When entity management fails to satisfy legal or regulatory requirements to report such information to external parties specified in law or regulation, auditors should first communicate the failure to report such information to those charged with governance. If the audited entity still does not report this information to the specified external parties as soon as practicable after the auditors' communication with those charged with governance, then the auditors should report the information directly to the specified external parties.

b. When entity management fails to take timely and appropriate steps to respond to known or likely fraud, noncompliance with provisions of laws, regulations, contracts, or grant agreements, or abuse that (1) is likely to have a material effect on the financial statements and (2) involves funding received directly or indirectly from a government agency, auditors should first report management's failure to take timely and appropriate steps to those charged with governance. If the audited entity still does not take timely and appropriate steps as soon as practicable after the auditors' communication with those charged with governance, then the auditors should report the entity's failure to take timely and appropriate steps directly to the funding agency.

4.31 The reporting in paragraph 4.30 is in addition to any legal requirements to report such information directly to parties outside the audited entity. Auditors should comply with these requirements even if they have resigned or been dismissed from the audit prior to its completion.

4.32 Auditors should obtain sufficient, appropriate evidence, such as confirmation from outside parties, to corroborate assertions by management of the audited entity that it has reported such findings in accordance with laws, regulations, or funding agreements. When auditors are unable to do so, they should report such information directly as discussed in paragraphs 4.30 and 4.31.

Reporting Views of Responsible Officials

4.33 When performing a GAGAS financial audit, if the auditors' report discloses deficiencies in internal control, fraud, noncompliance with provisions of laws, regulations, contracts, or grant agreements, or abuse, auditors should obtain and report the views of responsible officials of the audited entity concerning the findings, conclusions, and recommendations, as well as any planned corrective actions.

4.34 Providing a draft report with findings for review and comment by responsible officials of the audited entity and others helps the auditors develop a report that is fair, complete, and objective. Including the views of responsible officials results in a report that presents not only the auditors' findings, conclusions, and recommendations, but also the perspectives of the responsible officials of the audited entity and the corrective actions they plan to take. Obtaining the comments in writing is preferred, but oral comments are acceptable.

4.35 When auditors receive written comments from the responsible officials, they should include in their report a copy of the officials' written comments, or a summary of the comments received. When the responsible officials provide oral comments only, auditors should prepare a summary of the oral comments and provide a copy of the summary to the responsible officials to verify that the comments are accurately stated.

4.36 Auditors should also include in the report an evaluation of the comments, as appropriate. In cases in which the audited entity provides technical comments in addition to its written or oral comments on the report, auditors may disclose in the report that such comments were received.

4.37 Obtaining oral comments may be appropriate when, for example, there is a reporting date critical to meeting a user's needs; auditors have worked closely with the responsible officials throughout the work and the parties are familiar with the findings and issues addressed in the draft report; or the auditors do not expect major disagreements with findings, conclusions, or recommendations in the draft report, or major controversies with regard to the issues discussed in the draft report.

4.38 When the audited entity's comments are inconsistent or in conflict with the findings, conclusions, or recommendations in the draft report, or when planned corrective actions do not adequately address the auditors' recommendations, the auditors should evaluate the validity of the audited entity's comments. If the auditors disagree with the comments, they should explain in the report their reasons for disagreement. Conversely, the auditors should modify their report as necessary if they find the comments valid and supported with sufficient, appropriate evidence.

4.39 If the audited entity refuses to provide comments or is unable to provide comments within a reasonable period of time, the auditors may issue the report without receiving comments from the audited entity. In such cases, the auditors should indicate in the report that the audited entity did not provide comments.

Reporting Confidential and Sensitive Information

4.40 When performing a GAGAS financial audit, if certain pertinent information is prohibited from public disclosure or is excluded from a report due to the confidential or sensitive nature of the information, auditors should disclose in the report that certain information has been omitted and the reason or other circumstances that make the omission necessary.

4.41 Certain information may be classified or may otherwise be prohibited from general disclosure by federal, state, or local laws or regulations. In such circumstances, auditors may issue a separate, classified, or limited use report containing such information and distribute the report only to persons authorized by law or regulation to receive it.

4.42 Additional circumstances associated with public safety, privacy, or security concerns could also justify the exclusion of certain information from a publicly available or widely distributed report. For example, detailed information related to computer security for a particular program may be excluded from publicly available reports because of the potential damage that could be caused by the misuse of this information. In such circumstances, auditors may issue a limited use report containing such information and distribute the report only to those parties responsible for acting on the auditors' recommendations. In some instances, it may be appropriate to issue both a publicly available report with the sensitive information excluded and a limited use report. The auditors may consult with legal counsel regarding any requirements or other circumstances that may necessitate the omission of certain information.

4.43 Considering the broad public interest in the program or activity under audit assists auditors when deciding whether to exclude certain information from publicly available reports. When circumstances call for omission of certain information, auditors should evaluate whether this omission could distort the audit results or conceal improper or illegal practices.

4.44 When audit organizations are subject to public records laws, auditors should determine whether public records laws could impact the availability of classified or limited use reports and determine whether other means of communicating with management and those charged with governance would be more appropriate. For example, the auditors may communicate general information in a written report and communicate detailed information orally. The auditors may consult with legal counsel regarding applicable public records laws.

Distributing Reports

4.45 Distribution of reports completed in accordance with GAGAS depends on the relationship of the auditors to the audited organization and the nature of the information contained in the report. Auditors should document any limitation on report distribution.[74] The following discussion outlines distribution for reports completed in accordance with GAGAS:

---

[74]See paragraphs 4.41 and 4.42 for discussion of limited use reports containing confidential or sensitive information.

a. Audit organizations in government entities should distribute auditors' reports to those charged with governance, to the appropriate audited entity officials, and to the appropriate oversight bodies or organizations requiring or arranging for the audits. As appropriate, auditors should also distribute copies of the reports to other officials who have legal oversight authority or who may be responsible for acting on audit findings and recommendations, and to others authorized to receive such reports.

b. Internal audit organizations in government entities may also follow the Institute of Internal Auditors (IIA) *International Standards for the Professional Practice of Internal Auditing.*[75] In accordance with GAGAS and IIA standards, the head of the internal audit organization should communicate results to the parties who can ensure that the results are given due consideration. If not otherwise mandated by statutory or regulatory requirements, prior to releasing results to parties outside the organization, the head of the internal audit organization should: (1) assess the potential risk to the organization, (2) consult with senior management or legal counsel as appropriate, and (3) control dissemination by indicating the intended users in the report.

c. Public accounting firms contracted to perform an audit in accordance with GAGAS should clarify report distribution responsibilities with the engaging organization. If the contracting firm is responsible for the distribution, it should reach agreement with the party contracting for the audit about which officials or

---

[75]See paragraph 2.21 for additional discussion about using the IIA standards in conjunction with GAGAS and paragraph 2.22 for additional discussion about citing compliance with another set of standards.

organizations will receive the report and the steps being
taken to make the report available to the public.

Additional GAGAS Considerations for Financial Audits

4.46 Due to the objectives and public accountability of
GAGAS audits, additional considerations for financial
audits completed in accordance with GAGAS may
apply. These considerations relate to

a. materiality in GAGAS financial audits; and

b. early communication of deficiencies.[76]

Materiality in GAGAS Financial Audits

4.47 The AICPA standards require the auditor to apply
the concept of materiality appropriately in planning and
performing the audit.[77] Additional considerations may
apply to GAGAS financial audits of government entities
or entities that receive government awards. For
example, in audits performed in accordance with
GAGAS, auditors may find it appropriate to use lower
materiality levels as compared with the materiality
levels used in non-GAGAS audits because of the public
accountability of government entities and entities
receiving government funding, various legal and
regulatory requirements, and the visibility and sensitivity
of government programs.

---

[76]See paragraphs 4.47 through 4.48 for additional discussion of
paragraph 4.46 a-b.

[77]See AICPA AU-C Section 320, *Materiality in Planning and
Performing an Audit.*

Early Communication of Deficiencies

4.48 For some matters, early communication to those charged with governance or management may be important because of the relative significance and the urgency for corrective follow-up action.[78] Further, when a control deficiency results in noncompliance with provisions of laws, regulations, contracts, or grant agreements, or abuse, early communication is important to allow management to take prompt corrective action to prevent further noncompliance. When a deficiency is communicated early, the reporting requirements in paragraphs 4.19 through 4.23 still apply.

---

[78]See AICPA AU-C Section 265, *Communicating Internal Control Related Matters Identified in an Audit.*

Chapter 5

Standards for Attestation Engagements

Introduction	**5.01** This chapter contains requirements, guidance, and considerations for performing and reporting on attestation engagements conducted in accordance with generally accepted government auditing standards (GAGAS). Auditors performing attestation engagements in accordance with GAGAS should comply with the American Institute of Certified Public Accountants (AICPA) general attestation standard on criteria, the field work and reporting attestation standards, and the corresponding statements on standards for attestation engagements (SSAEs), which are incorporated in this chapter by reference.[79] Auditors performing attestation engagements in accordance with GAGAS should also comply with the additional requirements in this chapter. The requirements and guidance contained in chapters 1 through 3 also apply to attestation engagements performed in accordance with GAGAS.
	5.02 An attestation engagement can provide one of three levels of service as defined by the AICPA, namely an examination engagement, a review engagement, or an agreed-upon procedures engagement.[80] Auditors performing an attestation engagement should determine which of the three levels of service apply to that engagement and refer to the appropriate AICPA standards and GAGAS section below for applicable requirements and considerations.

---

[79]See AICPA AT Section 50, *SSAE Hierarchy.*

[80]See paragraph 2.09 and AICPA AT Section 101, *Attest Engagements.*

Examination Engagements

Additional Field Work Requirements for Examination Engagements

5.03 GAGAS establishes field work requirements for performing examination engagements in addition to the requirements contained in the AICPA standards. Auditors should comply with these additional requirements, along with the relevant AICPA standards for examination attestation engagements, when citing GAGAS in their examination reports. The additional field work requirements relate to:

a. auditor communication;

b. previous audits and attestation engagements;

c. fraud, noncompliance with provisions of laws, regulations, contracts, and grant agreements, and abuse;

d. developing elements of a finding; and

e. examination engagement documentation.[81]

Auditor Communication

5.04 In addition to the AICPA requirements for auditor communication,[82] when performing a GAGAS examination engagement, auditors should communicate pertinent information that in the auditors' professional judgment needs to be communicated to individuals contracting for or requesting the examination engagement, and to cognizant legislative committees

---

[81]See paragraphs 5.04 through 5.17 for additional discussion of 5.03 a-e.

[82]See AICPA AT Section 101.14 and 101.46, *Attest Engagements.*

when auditors perform the examination engagement pursuant to a law or regulation, or they conduct the work for the legislative committee that has oversight of the audited entity.

5.05 In those situations where there is not a single individual or group that both oversees the strategic direction of the audited entity and the fulfillment of its accountability obligations or in other situations where the identity of those charged with governance is not clearly evident, auditors should document the process followed and conclusions reached for identifying the appropriate individuals to receive the required auditor communications.

Previous Audits and Attestation Engagements

5.06 When performing a GAGAS examination engagement, auditors should evaluate whether the audited entity has taken appropriate corrective action to address findings and recommendations from previous engagements that could have a material effect on the subject matter, or an assertion about the subject matter, of the examination engagement. When planning the engagement, auditors should ask audited entity management to identify previous audits, attestation engagements, and other studies that directly relate to the subject matter or an assertion about the subject matter of the examination engagement being undertaken, including whether related recommendations have been implemented. Auditors should use this information in assessing risk and determining the nature, timing, and extent of current work, including determining the extent to which testing the implementation of the corrective actions is applicable to the current examination engagement objectives.

Fraud, Noncompliance with Provisions of Laws, Regulations, Contracts, and Grant Agreements, and Abuse

5.07 In addition to the AICPA requirements concerning fraud,[83] when performing a GAGAS examination engagement, auditors should design the engagement to detect instances of fraud and noncompliance with provisions of laws, regulations, contracts, and grant agreements that may have a material effect on the subject matter or the assertion thereon of the examination engagement. Auditors should assess the risk and possible effects of fraud and noncompliance with provisions of laws, regulations, contracts, and grant agreements that could have a material effect on the subject matter or an assertion about the subject matter of the examination engagement. When risk factors are identified, auditors should document the risk factors identified, the auditors' response to those risk factors individually or in combination, and the auditors' conclusions.[84]

5.08 Abuse involves behavior that is deficient or improper when compared with behavior that a prudent person would consider a reasonable and necessary business practice given the facts and circumstances. Abuse also includes misuse of authority or position for personal financial interests or those of an immediate or close family member or business associate,[85] Abuse does not necessarily involve fraud, or noncompliance with provisions of laws, regulations, contracts, or grant agreements.

---

[83]See AICPA AT Sections 501.27, *An Examination of an Entity's Internal Control Over Financial Reporting That Is Integrated With an Audit of Its Financial Statements*, 601.33, *Compliance Attestation*, and 701.42, *Management's Discussion and Analysis*.

[84]See paragraphs A.09 through A.13 for additional discussion of indicators of fraud risk and significance of provisions of laws, regulations, and contracts and grant agreements.

[85]See A.08 for additional examples of abuse.

5.09 Because the determination of abuse is subjective, auditors are not required to detect abuse in examination engagements. However, as part of a GAGAS examination engagement, if auditors become aware of abuse that could be quantitatively or qualitatively material, auditors should apply procedures specifically directed to ascertain the potential effect on the subject matter, or the assertion thereon, or other data significant to the objective of the examination engagement. After performing additional work, auditors may discover that the abuse represents potential fraud or noncompliance with provisions of laws, regulations, contracts, or grant agreements.

5.10 Avoiding interference with investigations or legal proceedings is important in pursuing indications of fraud, noncompliance with provisions of laws, regulations, contracts, or grant agreements, or abuse. Laws, regulations, or policies may require auditors to report indications of certain types of fraud, noncompliance with provisions of laws, regulations, contracts, or grant agreements, or abuse to law enforcement or investigatory authorities before performing additional audit procedures. When investigations or legal proceedings are initiated or in process, auditors should evaluate the impact on the current examination engagement. In some cases, it may be appropriate for the auditors to work with investigators or legal authorities, or withdraw from or defer further work on the examination engagement or a portion of the examination engagement to avoid interfering with an ongoing investigation or legal proceeding.

Developing Elements of a Finding

5.11 In an examination engagement, findings may involve deficiencies in internal control; noncompliance with provisions of laws, regulations, contracts, or grant agreements; fraud; or abuse. As part of a GAGAS examination engagement, when auditors identify findings, auditors should plan and perform procedures to develop the elements of the findings that are relevant and necessary to achieve the examination engagement objectives. The elements of a finding are discussed in paragraphs 5.12 through 5.15 below.

5.12 Criteria: The laws, regulations, contracts, grant agreements, standards, measures, expected performance, defined business practices, and benchmarks against which performance is compared or evaluated. Criteria identify the required or desired state or expectation with respect to the program or operation. Criteria provide a context for evaluating evidence and understanding the findings.

5.13 Condition: Condition is a situation that exists. The condition is determined and documented during the engagement.

5.14 Cause: The cause identifies the reason or explanation for the condition or the factor or factors responsible for the difference between the situation that exists (condition) and the required or desired state (criteria), which may also serve as a basis for recommendations for corrective actions. Common factors include poorly designed policies, procedures, or criteria; inconsistent, incomplete, or incorrect implementation; or factors beyond the control of program management. Auditors may assess whether the evidence provides a reasonable and convincing argument for why the stated cause is the key factor or factors contributing to the difference between the condition and the criteria.

5.15 Effect or potential effect: The effect is a clear, logical link to establish the impact or potential impact of the difference between the situation that exists (condition) and the required or desired state (criteria). The effect or potential effect identifies the outcomes or consequences of the condition. When the engagement objectives include identifying the actual or potential consequences of a condition that varies (either positively or negatively) from the criteria identified in the engagement, "effect" is a measure of those consequences. Effect or potential effect may be used to demonstrate the need for corrective action in response to identified problems or relevant risks.

Examination Engagement Documentation	**5.16** In addition to AICPA requirements for audit documentation,[86] auditors should comply with the following additional requirements when performing a GAGAS examination engagement.[87]

a. Prepare attest documentation in sufficient detail to enable an experienced auditor, having no previous connection to the examination engagement, to understand from the documentation the nature, timing, extent, and results of procedures performed and the evidence obtained and its source and the conclusions reached, including evidence that supports the auditors' significant judgments and conclusions. An experienced auditor means an individual (whether internal or external to the audit organization) who possesses the competencies and skills to be able to perform the examination engagement. These competencies and skills include an understanding of (1) examination engagement processes and related SSAEs,[88] (2) GAGAS and applicable legal and regulatory requirements, (3) the subject matter that the auditors are engaged to report on, (4) the suitability and

---

[86]See AICPA AT Section 101.100–101.107, *Attest Engagements.*

[87]See paragraphs 5.05, 5.07, 5.25, and 5.44 for additional documentation requirements regarding attestation engagements.

[88]See paragraphs 3.74 and 3.75 for additional discussion of qualifications for attestation engagements.

availability of criteria, and (5) issues related to the
audited entity's environment.

b. Document supervisory review, before the date of the
examination report, of the evidence that supports
findings, conclusions, and recommendations contained
in the examination report.

c. Document any departures from the GAGAS
requirements and the impact on the engagement and
on the auditors' conclusions when the examination
engagement is not in compliance with applicable
GAGAS requirements due to law, regulation, scope
limitations, restrictions on access to records, or other
issues impacting the audit. This applies to departures
from unconditional requirements and from
presumptively mandatory requirements when
alternative procedures performed in the circumstances
were not sufficient to achieve the objectives of the
requirement.[89]

5.17 When performing GAGAS examination
engagements and subject to applicable laws and
regulations, auditors should make appropriate
individuals, as well as attest documentation, available
upon request and in a timely manner to other auditors
or reviewers. Underlying GAGAS engagements is the
premise that audit organizations in federal, state, and
local governments and public accounting firms engaged
to perform an engagement in accordance with GAGAS
cooperate in performing examination engagements of
programs of common interest so that auditors may use
others' work and avoid duplication of efforts. The use of
auditors' work by other auditors may be facilitated by
contractual arrangements for GAGAS engagements

---

[89]See paragraph 2.15 for a definition of GAGAS requirements.

that provide for full and timely access to appropriate individuals, as well as attest documentation.

Additional GAGAS Reporting Requirements for Examination Engagements

5.18 In addition to the AICPA requirements for reporting on examination engagements,[90] auditors should comply with the following additional requirements when citing GAGAS in their examination reports. The additional reporting requirements relate to

a. reporting auditors' compliance with GAGAS;

b. reporting deficiencies in internal control, fraud, noncompliance with provisions of laws, regulations, contracts, and grant agreements, and abuse;

c. reporting views of responsible officials;

d. reporting confidential or sensitive information; and

e. distributing reports.[91]

Reporting Auditors' Compliance with GAGAS

5.19 When auditors comply with all applicable GAGAS requirements for examination engagements, they should include a statement in the examination report that they performed the examination engagement in accordance with GAGAS.[92] Because GAGAS incorporates by reference the AICPA's general attestation standard on criteria, the field work and reporting attestation standards, and the corresponding SSAEs, GAGAS does not require auditors to cite

---

[90]See AICPA AT Section 101.63-101.87, *Attest Engagements*.

[91]See paragraphs 5.19 through 5.44 for additional discussion of paragraph 5.18 a-e.

[92]See paragraphs 2.24 and 2.25 for additional requirements on citing compliance with GAGAS.

compliance with the AICPA standards when citing
compliance with GAGAS. GAGAS does not prohibit
auditors from issuing a separate report conforming only
to the requirements of AICPA or other standards.[93]

Reporting Deficiencies in Internal Control, Fraud, Noncompliance with Provisions of Laws, Regulations, Contracts, and Grant Agreements, and Abuse

5.20 When performing GAGAS examination
engagements, auditors should report, based upon the
work performed, (1) significant deficiencies and material
weaknesses in internal control;[94] (2) instances of fraud[95]
and noncompliance with provisions of laws or
regulations that have a material effect on the subject
matter or an assertion about the subject matter and any
other instances that warrant the attention of those
charged with governance; (3) noncompliance with
provisions of contracts or grant agreements that has a
material effect on the subject matter or an assertion
about the subject matter of the examination
engagement; and (4) abuse that has a material effect
on the subject matter or an assertion about the subject
matter of the examination engagement. Auditors should
include this information either in the same or in separate
report(s).

5.21 If auditors report separately (including separate
reports bound in the same document) on the items
discussed in paragraph 5.20, they should state in the
examination report that they are issuing those additional
reports. They should include a reference to the separate
reports and also state that the reports are an integral
part of a GAGAS examination engagement.

---

[93]See AICPA AT Sections 101.85e, *Attest Engagements.*

[94]See paragraph A.06 for examples of deficiencies in internal control.

[95]See paragraph A.10 for examples of indicators of fraud risk.

Deficiencies in Internal
Control

5.22 In addition to the AICPA requirements concerning internal control,[96] when performing GAGAS examination engagements, including attestation engagements related to internal control,[97] auditors should include in the examination report all deficiencies, even those communicated early,[98] that are considered to be significant deficiencies or material weaknesses.

5.23 Determining whether and how to communicate to officials of the audited entity internal control deficiencies that warrant the attention of those charged with governance, but are not considered significant deficiencies or material weaknesses, is a matter of professional judgment.

Fraud, Noncompliance
with Provisions of
Laws, Regulations,
Contracts, and Grant
Agreements, and Abuse

5.24 When performing a GAGAS examination engagement, and auditors conclude, based on sufficient, appropriate evidence, that any of the following either has occurred or is likely to have occurred, they should include in their examination report the relevant information about

a. fraud[99] and noncompliance with provisions of laws or regulations that have a material effect on the subject matter or an assertion about the subject matter and any other instances that warrant the attention of those charged with governance,

---

[96]See AICPA AT Section 101.52 through 101.53, *Attest Engagements.*

[97]See AICPA AT Section 501.07, *An Examination of an Entity's Internal Control Over Financial Reporting That Is Integrated With an Audit of Its Financial Statements.*

[98]See paragraph 5.47 for a discussion of early communication of deficiencies.

[99]See paragraph A.10 for examples of indicators of fraud risk.

b. noncompliance with provisions of contracts or grant agreements that has a material effect on the subject matter or an assertion about the subject matter, or

c. abuse[100] that is material to the subject matter or an assertion about the subject matter, either quantitatively or qualitatively.[101]

5.25 When auditors detect instances of noncompliance with provisions of contracts or grant agreements, or abuse that have an effect on the subject matter or an assertion about the subject matter that are less than material but warrant the attention of those charged with governance, they should communicate those findings in writing to audited entity officials. When auditors detect any instances of fraud, noncompliance with provisions of laws, regulations, contracts, or grant agreements, or abuse that do not warrant the attention of those charged with governance, the auditors' determination of whether and how to communicate such instances to audited entity officials is a matter of professional judgment.

5.26 When fraud, noncompliance with provisions of laws, regulations, contracts, or grant agreements, or abuse either have occurred or are likely to have occurred, auditors may consult with authorities or legal counsel about whether publicly reporting such information would compromise investigative or legal proceedings. Auditors may limit their public reporting to matters that would not compromise those proceedings and, for example, report only on information that is already a part of the public record.

---

[100]See paragraph A.08 for examples of abuse.

[101]See paragraphs 5.08 and 5.09 for a discussion of abuse.

Presenting Findings in the Examination Report

5.27 When performing a GAGAS examination engagement and presenting findings such as deficiencies in internal control, fraud, noncompliance with provisions of laws, regulations, contracts, or grant agreements, or abuse, auditors should develop the elements of the findings to the extent necessary. Clearly developed findings, as discussed in paragraphs 5.11 through 5.15, assist management or oversight officials of the audited entity in understanding the need for taking corrective action, and assist auditors in making recommendations for corrective action. If auditors sufficiently develop the elements of a finding, they may provide recommendations for corrective action.

5.28 Auditors should place their findings in perspective by describing the nature and extent of the issues being reported and the extent of the work performed that resulted in the finding. To give the reader a basis for judging the prevalence and consequences of these findings, auditors should, as appropriate, relate the instances identified to the population or the number of cases examined and quantify the results in terms of dollar value or other measures. If the results cannot be projected, auditors should limit their conclusions appropriately.

Reporting Findings Directly to Parties Outside the Audited Entity

5.29 Auditors should report known or likely fraud, noncompliance with provisions of laws, regulations, contracts, or grant agreements, or abuse directly to parties outside the audited entity in the following two circumstances.

a. When entity management fails to satisfy legal or regulatory requirements to report such information to external parties specified in law or regulation, auditors should first communicate the failure to report such information to those charged with governance. If the audited entity still does not report this information to the specified external parties as soon as practicable after the auditors' communication with those charged with governance, then the auditors should report the information directly to the specified external parties.

b. When entity management fails to take timely and appropriate steps to respond to known or likely fraud, noncompliance with provisions of laws, regulations, contracts, or grant agreements, or abuse that (1) is likely to have a material effect on the subject matter or an assertion about the subject matter and (2) involves funding received directly or indirectly from a government agency, auditors should first report management's failure to take timely and appropriate steps to those charged with governance. If the audited entity still does not take timely and appropriate steps as soon as practicable after the auditors' communication with those charged with governance, then the auditors should report the entity's failure to take timely and appropriate steps directly to the funding agency.

5.30 The reporting in paragraph 5.29 is in addition to any legal requirements to report such information directly to parties outside the audited entity. Auditors should comply with these requirements even if they have resigned or been dismissed from the engagement prior to its completion.

5.31 Auditors should obtain sufficient, appropriate evidence, such as confirmation from outside parties, to corroborate assertions by management of the audited entity that it has reported such findings in accordance with laws, regulations, or funding agreements. When auditors are unable to do so, they should report such information directly as discussed in paragraph 5.29.

Reporting Views of Responsible Officials

5.32 When performing a GAGAS examination engagement, if the examination report discloses deficiencies in internal control, fraud, noncompliance with provisions of laws, regulations, contracts, or grant agreements, or abuse, auditors should obtain and report the views of responsible officials of the audited entity concerning the findings, conclusions, and recommendations, as well as any planned corrective actions.

5.33 Providing a draft report with findings for review and comment by responsible officials of the audited entity and others helps the auditors develop a report that is fair, complete, and objective. Including the views of responsible officials results in a report that presents not only the auditors' findings, conclusions, and recommendations, but also the perspectives of the responsible officials of the audited entity and the corrective actions they plan to take. Obtaining the comments in writing is preferred, but oral comments are acceptable.

5.34 When auditors receive written comments from the responsible officials, they should include in their report a copy of the officials' written comments, or a summary of the comments received. When the responsible officials provide oral comments only, auditors should prepare a summary of the oral comments and provide a copy of the summary to the responsible officials to verify that the comments are accurately stated.

5.35 Auditors should also include in the report an evaluation of the comments, as appropriate. In cases in which the audited entity provides technical comments in addition to its written or oral comments on the report, auditors may disclose in the report that such comments were received.

5.36 Obtaining oral comments may be appropriate when, for example, there is a reporting date critical to meeting a user's needs; auditors have worked closely with the responsible officials throughout the work and the parties are familiar with the findings and issues addressed in the draft report; or the auditors do not expect major disagreements with findings, conclusions, or recommendations in the draft report, or major controversies with regard to the issues discussed in the draft report.

5.37 When the audited entity's comments are inconsistent or in conflict with the findings, conclusions, or recommendations in the draft report, or when planned corrective actions do not adequately address the auditors' recommendations, the auditors should evaluate the validity of the audited entity's comments. If the auditors disagree with the comments, they should explain in the report their reasons for disagreement. Conversely, the auditors should modify their report as necessary if they find the comments valid and supported with sufficient, appropriate evidence.

5.38 If the audited entity refuses to provide comments or is unable to provide comments within a reasonable period of time, the auditors may issue the report without receiving comments from the audited entity. In such cases, the auditors should indicate in the report that the audited entity did not provide comments.

Reporting Confidential and Sensitive Information

5.39 When performing a GAGAS examination engagement, if certain pertinent information is prohibited from public disclosure or is excluded from a report due to the confidential or sensitive nature of the information, auditors should disclose in the report that certain information has been omitted and the reason or other circumstances that make the omission necessary.

5.40 Certain information may be classified or may be otherwise prohibited from general disclosure by federal, state, or local laws or regulations. In such circumstances, auditors may issue a separate classified or limited use report containing such information and distribute the report only to persons authorized by law or regulation to receive it.

5.41 Additional circumstances associated with public safety, privacy, or security concerns could also justify the exclusion of certain information from a publicly available or widely distributed report. For example, detailed information related to computer security for a particular program may be excluded from publicly available reports because of the potential damage that could be caused by the misuse of this information. In such circumstances, auditors may issue a limited use report containing such information and distribute the report only to those parties responsible for acting on the auditors' recommendations. In some instances, it may be appropriate to issue both a publicly available report with the sensitive information excluded and a limited use report. The auditors may consult with legal counsel regarding any requirements or other circumstances that may necessitate the omission of certain information.

5.42 Considering the broad public interest in the program or activity under review assists auditors when deciding whether to exclude certain information from publicly available reports. When circumstances call for omission of certain information, auditors should evaluate whether this omission could distort the examination engagement results or conceal improper or illegal practices.

5.43 When audit organizations are subject to public records laws, auditors should determine whether public records laws could impact the availability of classified or limited use reports and determine whether other means of communicating with management and those charged with governance would be more appropriate. For example, the auditors may communicate general information in a written report and communicate detailed information orally. The auditors may consult with legal counsel regarding applicable public records laws.

Distributing Reports

5.44 Distribution of reports completed in accordance with GAGAS depends on the relationship of the auditors to the audited organization and the nature of the information contained in the report. Auditors should document any limitation on report distribution.[102] The following discussion outlines distribution for reports completed in accordance with GAGAS:

a. Audit organizations in government entities should distribute reports to those charged with governance, to the appropriate audited entity officials, and to the appropriate oversight bodies or organizations requiring or arranging for the engagements. As appropriate, auditors should also distribute copies of the reports to other officials who have legal oversight authority or who may be responsible for acting on engagement findings and recommendations, and to others authorized to receive such reports.

b. Internal audit organizations in government entities may also follow the Institute of Internal Auditors (IIA) *International Standards for the Professional Practice of Internal Auditing.*[103] In accordance with GAGAS and IIA standards, the head of the internal audit organization should communicate results to the parties who can ensure that the results are given due consideration. If not otherwise mandated by statutory or regulatory

---

[102]See paragraphs 5.40 and 5.41 for discussion of limited use reports containing confidential or sensitive information.

[103]See paragraph 2.21 for additional discussion about using the IIA standards in conjunction with GAGAS and paragraph 2.22 for additional discussion about citing compliance with another set of standards.

requirements, prior to releasing results to parties outside the organization, the head of the internal audit organization should: (1) assess the potential risk to the organization, (2) consult with senior management or legal counsel as appropriate, and (3) control dissemination by indicating the intended users in the report.

c. Public accounting firms contracted to perform an examination engagement in accordance with GAGAS should clarify report distribution responsibilities with the engaging organization. If the contracting firm is responsible for the distribution, it should reach agreement with the party contracting for the engagement about which officials or organizations will receive the report and the steps being taken to make the report available to the public.

Additional GAGAS Considerations for Examination Engagements

5.45 Due to the objectives and public accountability of GAGAS examination engagements, additional considerations for examination engagements completed in accordance with GAGAS may apply. These considerations relate to

a. Materiality in GAGAS examination engagements, and

b. Early communication of deficiencies.[104]

Materiality in GAGAS Examination Engagements

5.46 The AICPA standards require that one of the factors to be considered when planning an attest engagement includes preliminary judgments about attestation risk and materiality for attest purposes.[105]

---

[104]See paragraphs 5.46 and 5.47 for additional discussion of paragraph 5.45 a-b.

[105]See AICPA AT Section 101.45b and 101.67, *Attest Engagements.*

Additional considerations may apply to GAGAS examination engagements of government entities or entities that receive government awards. For example, in engagements performed in accordance with GAGAS, auditors may find it appropriate to use lower materiality levels as compared with the materiality levels used in non-GAGAS engagements because of the public accountability of government entities and entities receiving government funding, various legal and regulatory requirements, and the visibility and sensitivity of government programs.

Early Communication of Deficiencies

5.47 For some matters, early communication to those charged with governance or management may be important because of the relative significance and the urgency for corrective follow-up action.[106] Further, when a control deficiency results in noncompliance with provisions of laws, regulations, contracts, or grant agreements, or abuse, early communication is important to allow management to take prompt corrective action to prevent further noncompliance. When a deficiency is communicated early, the reporting requirements in paragraph 5.20 still apply.

[106]See AICPA AT Section 501.103, *An Examination of an Entity's Internal Control Over Financial Reporting That Is Integrated With an Audit of Its Financial Statements.*

Review Engagements

Additional GAGAS Field Work Requirements for Review Engagements

5.48 GAGAS establishes a field work requirement for review engagements in addition to the requirements contained in the AICPA standards. Auditors should comply with this additional requirement, along with the relevant AICPA standards for review engagements, when citing GAGAS in their review engagement reports. The additional requirement relates to communicating significant deficiencies, material weaknesses, instances of fraud, noncompliance with provisions of laws, regulations, contracts, or grant agreements, or abuse that come to the auditors' attention during a review engagement.

Communicating Significant Deficiencies, Material Weaknesses, Instances of Fraud, Noncompliance with Provisions of Laws, Regulations, Contracts, and Grant Agreements, and Abuse

5.49 If, on the basis of conducting the procedures necessary to perform a review, significant deficiencies; material weaknesses; instances of fraud, noncompliance with provisions of laws, regulations, contracts, or grant agreements; or abuse come to the auditors' attention that warrant the attention of those charged with governance, GAGAS requires that auditors should communicate such matters to audited entity officials. When auditors detect any instances of fraud, noncompliance with provisions of laws, regulations, contracts, or grant agreements, or abuse that do not warrant the attention of those charged with governance, the auditors' determination of whether and how to communicate such instances to audited entity officials is a matter of professional judgment. Additionally, auditors should determine whether the existence of such matters affects the auditors' ability to conduct or report on the review.

Additional GAGAS Reporting Requirements for Review Engagements

5.50 GAGAS establishes reporting requirements for review engagements in addition to the requirements contained in the AICPA standards.[107] Auditors should comply with these additional requirements when citing GAGAS in their review engagement reports. The additional requirements relate to

a. reporting auditors' compliance with GAGAS; and

b. distributing reports.[108]

Reporting Auditors' Compliance with GAGAS

5.51 When auditors comply with all applicable requirements for a review engagement conducted in accordance with GAGAS, they should include a statement in the review report that they performed the engagement in accordance with GAGAS.[109] Because GAGAS incorporates by reference the general standard on criteria, and the field work and reporting standards of the AICPA SSAEs, GAGAS does not require auditors to cite compliance with the AICPA standards when citing compliance with GAGAS. GAGAS does not prohibit auditors from issuing a separate report conforming only to the requirements of AICPA or other standards.[110]

Distributing Reports

5.52 Distribution of reports completed in accordance with GAGAS depends on the relationship of the auditors to the audited organization and the nature of the

---

[107]See AICPA AT Section 101.63-101.83 and 101.88-101.90, *Attest Engagements*.

[108]See paragraphs 5.51 and 5.52 for additional discussion of paragraph 5.50 a-b.

[109]See paragraphs 2.24 and 2.25 for additional requirements on citing compliance with GAGAS.

[110]See AICPA AT Section 101.89d, *Attest Engagements*.

information contained in the report. For GAGAS review engagements, if the subject matter or the assertion involves material that is classified for security purposes or contains confidential or sensitive information, auditors should limit the report distribution. Auditors should document any limitation on report distribution. The following discussion outlines distribution for reports completed in accordance with GAGAS:

a. Audit organizations in government entities should distribute reports to those charged with governance, to the appropriate audited entity officials, and to the appropriate oversight bodies or organizations requiring or arranging for the engagements. As appropriate, auditors should also distribute copies of the reports to other officials who have legal oversight authority, and to others authorized to receive such reports.

b. Internal audit organizations in government entities may also follow the Institute of Internal Auditors (IIA) *International Standards for the Professional Practice of Internal Auditing.*[111] In accordance with GAGAS and IIA standards, the head of the internal audit organization should communicate results to the parties who can ensure that the results are given due consideration. If not otherwise mandated by statutory or regulatory requirements, prior to releasing results to parties outside the organization, the head of the internal audit organization should: (1) assess the potential risk to the organization, (2) consult with senior management or legal counsel as appropriate, and (3) control dissemination by indicating the intended users in the report.

---

[111]See paragraph 2.21 for additional discussion about using the IIA standards in conjunction with GAGAS and paragraph 2.22 for additional discussion about citing compliance with another set of standards.

c. Public accounting firms contracted to perform a review engagement in accordance with GAGAS should clarify report distribution responsibilities with the engaging organization. If the contracting firm is responsible for the distribution, it should reach agreement with the party contracting for the engagement about which officials or organizations will receive the report and the steps being taken to make the report available to the public.

Additional GAGAS Considerations for Review Engagements

5.53 Due to the objectives and public accountability of GAGAS review engagements, additional considerations for review engagements performed in accordance with GAGAS may apply. These considerations relate to

a. establishing an understanding regarding services to be performed; and

b. reporting on review engagements.[112]

Establishing an Understanding Regarding Services to be Performed

5.54 The AICPA standards require auditors to establish an understanding with the audited entity (client) regarding the services to be performed for each attestation engagement. Such an understanding reduces the risk that either the auditors (practitioner) or the audited entity may misinterpret the needs or expectations of the other party. The understanding includes the objectives of the engagement, responsibilities of entity management, responsibilities of auditors, and limitations of the engagement.[113]

---

[112]See paragraphs 5.54 through 5.57 for additional discussion of 5.53 a-b.

[113]See AICPA AT Section 101.46, *Attest Engagements*.

5.55 Auditors often perform GAGAS engagements under a contract with a party other than the officials of the audited entity or pursuant to a third-party request. In such cases, auditors may also find it appropriate to communicate information regarding the services to be performed to the individuals contracting for or requesting the engagement. Such an understanding can help auditors avoid any misunderstandings regarding the nature of the review engagement. For example, review engagements only provide a moderate level of assurance expressed as a conclusion in the form of negative assurance, and, as a result, auditors do not perform sufficient work to be able to develop elements of a finding or provide recommendations that are common in other types of GAGAS engagements. Under such circumstances, for example, requesting parties may find that a different type of attestation engagement or a performance audit may provide the appropriate level of assurance to meet their needs.

Reporting on Review Engagements

5.56 The AICPA standards require that the auditors' review report be in the form of a conclusion expressed in the form of negative assurance.[114]

5.57 Because reviews are substantially less in scope than audits and examination engagements, it is important to include all required reporting elements contained in the SSAEs.[115] For example, a required element of the review report is a statement that a review engagement is substantially less in scope than an examination, the objective of which is an expression of opinion on the subject matter, and accordingly, review reports express no such opinion. Including only those elements that the AICPA reporting standards for review

---

[114]See AICPA AT Section 101.68, *Attest Engagements.*

[115]See AICPA AT Section 101.89, *Attest Engagements.*

engagements require or permit ensures that auditors comply with the AICPA standards and that users of GAGAS reports have an understanding of the nature of the work performed and the results of the review engagement.

Agreed-Upon Procedures Engagements

Additional GAGAS Field Work Requirements for Agreed-Upon Procedures Engagements

5.58 GAGAS establishes a field work requirement for agreed-upon procedures engagements in addition to the requirements contained in the AICPA standards. Auditors should comply with this additional requirement, along with the relevant AICPA standards for agreed-upon procedures engagements, when citing GAGAS in their agreed-upon procedures engagement reports. The additional requirement relates to communicating significant deficiencies, material weaknesses, instances of fraud, noncompliance with provisions of laws, regulations, contracts, or grant agreements, or abuse that comes to the auditors' attention during an agreed-upon procedures engagement.

Communicating Significant Deficiencies, Material Weaknesses, Instances of Fraud, Noncompliance with Provisions of Laws, Regulations, Contracts, and Grant Agreements, and Abuse

5.59 If, on the basis of conducting the procedures necessary to perform an agreed-upon procedures engagement,[116] significant deficiencies, material weaknesses, instances of fraud, noncompliance with provisions of laws, regulations, contracts, or grant agreements, or abuse come to the auditors' attention that warrant the attention of those charged with governance, GAGAS requires that auditors should communicate such matters to audited entity officials. When auditors detect any instances of fraud, noncompliance with provisions of laws, regulations, contracts, or grant agreements, or abuse that do not warrant the attention of those charged with governance, the auditors' determination of whether and how to communicate such instances to audited entity officials is a matter of professional judgment. Additionally, auditors should determine whether the existence of such matters affects the auditors' ability to conduct or report on the agreed-upon procedures engagement.

Additional GAGAS Reporting Requirements for Agreed-Upon Procedures Engagements

5.60 GAGAS establishes reporting requirements for agreed-upon procedures engagements in addition to the requirements contained in the AICPA standards.[117] Auditors should comply with these additional requirements when citing GAGAS in their agreed-upon procedures engagement reports. The additional requirements relate to

a. reporting auditors' compliance with GAGAS; and

---

[116]See AICPA AT Section 201.03, *Agreed-Upon Procedures Engagements.*

[117]See AICPA AT Section 201.31-201.36, *Agreed-Upon Procedures Engagements.*

b. distributing reports.[118]

Reporting Auditors' Compliance with GAGAS

5.61 When auditors comply with all applicable GAGAS requirements for agreed-upon procedures engagements, they should include a statement in the agreed-upon procedures engagement report that they performed the engagement in accordance with GAGAS.[119] Because GAGAS incorporates by reference the AICPA's general attestation standard on criteria, the field work and reporting attestation standards, and the corresponding SSAEs, GAGAS does not require auditors to cite compliance with the AICPA standards when citing compliance with GAGAS. GAGAS does not prohibit auditors from issuing a separate report conforming only to the requirements of AICPA or other standards.[120]

Distributing Reports

5.62 Distribution of reports completed in accordance with GAGAS depends on the relationship of the auditors to the audited organization and the nature of the information contained in the report. For GAGAS agreed-upon procedures engagements, if the subject matter or the assertion involves material that is classified for security purposes or contains confidential or sensitive information, auditors should limit the report distribution. Auditors should document any limitation on report distribution. The following discussion outlines distribution for reports completed in accordance with GAGAS:

---

[118]See paragraphs 5.61 and 5.62 for additional discussion of paragraph 5.60 a-b.

[119]See paragraphs 2.24 and 2.25 for additional requirements on citing compliance with GAGAS.

[120]See AICPA AT Section 201.31 g, *Agreed-Upon Procedures Engagements.*

a. Audit organizations in government entities should distribute reports to those charged with governance, to the appropriate audited entity officials, and to the appropriate oversight bodies or organizations requiring or arranging for the engagements. As appropriate, auditors should also distribute copies of the reports to other officials who have legal oversight authority, and to others authorized to receive such reports.

b. Internal audit organizations in government entities may also follow the Institute of Internal Auditors (IIA) *International Standards for the Professional Practice of Internal Auditing.*[121] In accordance with GAGAS and IIA standards, the head of the internal audit organization should communicate results to the parties who can ensure that the results are given due consideration. If not otherwise mandated by statutory or regulatory requirements, prior to releasing results to parties outside the organization, the head of the internal audit organization should: (1) assess the potential risk to the organization, (2) consult with senior management or legal counsel as appropriate, and (3) control dissemination by indicating the intended users in the report.

c. Public accounting firms contracted to perform an agreed-upon procedures engagement in accordance with GAGAS should clarify report distribution responsibilities with the engaging organization. If the contracting firm is responsible for the distribution, it should reach agreement with the party contracting for the engagement about which officials or organizations will receive the report and the steps being taken to make the report available to the public.

---

[121]See paragraph 2.21 for additional discussion about using the IIA standards in conjunction with GAGAS and paragraph 2.22 for additional discussion about citing compliance with another set of standards.

Additional GAGAS Considerations for Agreed-Upon Procedures Engagements

5.63 Due to the objectives and public accountability of GAGAS agreed-upon procedures engagements, additional considerations for agreed-upon procedures engagements performed in accordance with GAGAS may apply. These considerations relate to

a. establishing an understanding regarding services to be performed; and

b. reporting on agreed-upon procedures engagements.[122]

Establishing an Understanding Regarding Services to be Performed

5.64 The AICPA standards require auditors to establish an understanding with the audited entity (client) regarding the services to be performed for each attestation engagement. Such an understanding reduces the risk that either the auditors (practitioner) or the audited entity may misinterpret the needs or expectations of the other party. The understanding includes the objectives of the engagement, responsibilities of entity management, responsibilities of auditors, and limitations of the engagement.[123]

5.65 Auditors often perform GAGAS engagements under a contract with a party other than the officials of the audited entity or pursuant to a third-party request. In such cases, auditors may also find it appropriate to communicate information regarding the services to be performed to the individuals contracting for or requesting the engagement. Such an understanding can help auditors avoid any misunderstandings regarding the nature of the agreed-upon procedures

---

[122]See paragraphs 5.64 through 5.67 for additional discussion of paragraph 5.63 a-b.

[123]See AICPA AT Sections 101.46, *Attest Engagements,* and 201.10, *Agreed-Upon Procedures Engagements.*

engagement. For example, agreed-upon procedures engagements provide neither a high nor moderate level of assurance, and, as a result, auditors do not perform sufficient work to be able to develop elements of a finding or provide recommendations that are common in other types of GAGAS engagements. Under such circumstances, for example, requesting parties may find that a different type of attestation engagement or a performance audit may provide the appropriate level of assurance to meet their needs.

Reporting on Agreed-Upon Procedures Engagements

5.66 The AICPA standards require that the auditors' report on agreed-upon procedures engagements be in the form of procedures and findings and specifies the required elements to be contained in the report.[124]

5.67 Because GAGAS agreed-upon procedures engagements are substantially less in scope than audits and examination engagements, it is important not to deviate from the required reporting elements contained in the SSAEs. For example, a required element of the report on agreed-upon procedures is a statement that the auditors were not engaged to and did not conduct an examination or a review of the subject matter, the objectives of which would be the expression of an opinion or limited assurance and that if the auditors had performed additional procedures, other matters might have come to their attention that would have been reported.[125] Another required element is a statement that the sufficiency of the procedures is solely the responsibility of the specified parties and a disclaimer of

---

[124]See AICPA AT Section 201.31, *Agreed-Upon Procedures Engagements*.

[125]See AICPA AT Section 201.31k, *Agreed-Upon Procedures Engagements*.

responsibility for the sufficiency of those procedures.[126] Including only those elements that the AICPA reporting standards for agreed-upon procedure engagements require or permit ensures that auditors comply with the AICPA standards and that users of GAGAS reports have an understanding of the nature of the work performed and the results of the agreed-upon procedures engagement.

---

[126]See AICPA AT Section 201.31h and 201.11-201.14, *Agreed-Upon Procedures Engagements.*

Chapter 6

Field Work Standards for Performance Audits

Introduction

6.01 This chapter contains field work requirements and guidance for performance audits conducted in accordance with generally accepted government auditing standards (GAGAS). The purpose of field work requirements is to establish an overall approach for auditors to apply in obtaining reasonable assurance that the evidence is sufficient and appropriate to support the auditors' findings and conclusions. The field work requirements for performance audits relate to planning the audit; supervising staff; obtaining sufficient, appropriate evidence; and preparing audit documentation. The concepts of reasonable assurance, significance, and audit risk form a framework for applying these requirements and are included throughout the discussion of performance audits.

6.02 For performance audits conducted in accordance with GAGAS, the requirements and guidance in chapters 1 through 3, 6, and 7 apply.

Reasonable Assurance

6.03 In performance audits that comply with GAGAS, auditors obtain reasonable assurance that evidence is sufficient and appropriate to support the auditors' findings and conclusions in relation to the audit objectives.[127] Thus, the sufficiency and appropriateness of evidence needed and tests of evidence will vary based on the audit objectives, findings, and conclusions. Objectives for performance audits range from narrow to broad and involve varying types and quality of evidence. In some engagements, sufficient, appropriate evidence is available, but in others, information may have limitations. Professional judgment assists auditors in determining the audit scope and methodology needed to address the audit objectives,

---

[127]See paragraphs 2.11 and A2.02 for additional discussion of performance audit objectives.

and in evaluating whether sufficient, appropriate evidence has been obtained to address the audit objectives.

Significance in a Performance Audit

6.04 The concept of significance assists auditors throughout a performance audit, including when deciding the type and extent of audit work to perform, when evaluating results of audit work, and when developing the report and related findings and conclusions. Significance is defined as the relative importance of a matter within the context in which it is being considered, including quantitative and qualitative factors. Such factors include the magnitude of the matter in relation to the subject matter of the audit, the nature and effect of the matter, the relevance of the matter, the needs and interests of an objective third party with knowledge of the relevant information, and the impact of the matter to the audited program or activity. Professional judgment assists auditors when evaluating the significance of matters within the context of the audit objectives. In the performance audit requirements, the term "significant" is comparable to the term "material" as used in the context of financial statement engagements.

Audit Risk

6.05 Audit risk is the possibility that the auditors' findings, conclusions, recommendations, or assurance may be improper or incomplete, as a result of factors such as evidence that is not sufficient and/or appropriate, an inadequate audit process, or intentional omissions or misleading information due to misrepresentation or fraud. The assessment of audit risk involves both qualitative and quantitative considerations. Factors impacting audit risk include the time frames, complexity, or sensitivity of the work; size of the program in terms of dollar amounts and number of citizens served; adequacy of the audited entity's systems and processes to detect inconsistencies, significant errors, or fraud; and auditors' access to records. Audit risk includes the risk that auditors will not detect a mistake, inconsistency, significant error, or fraud in the evidence supporting the audit. Audit risk can be reduced by taking actions such as increasing the scope of work; adding specialists, additional reviewers, and other resources to perform the audit; changing the methodology to obtain additional evidence, higher quality evidence, or alternative forms of corroborating evidence; or aligning the findings and conclusions to reflect the evidence obtained.

Planning

6.06 Auditors must adequately plan and document the planning of the work necessary to address the audit objectives.

6.07 Auditors must plan the audit to reduce audit risk to an appropriate level for the auditors to obtain reasonable assurance that the evidence is sufficient and appropriate[128] to support the auditors' findings and conclusions. This determination is a matter of professional judgment. In planning the audit, auditors should assess significance and audit risk and apply these assessments in defining the audit objectives and the scope and methodology to address those objectives. Planning is a continuous process throughout the audit. Therefore, auditors may need to adjust the audit objectives, scope, and methodology as work is being completed. In situations where the audit objectives are established by statute or legislative oversight, auditors may not have latitude to define or adjust the audit objectives or scope.

---

[128]See paragraphs 6.56 through 6.72 for a discussion about assessing the sufficiency and appropriateness of evidence.

6.08 The objectives are what the audit is intended to accomplish. They identify the audit subject matter and performance aspects to be included, and may also include the potential findings and reporting elements that the auditors expect to develop. Audit objectives can be thought of as questions about the program that the auditors seek to answer based on evidence obtained and assessed against criteria. The term "program" is used in GAGAS to include government entities, organizations, programs, activities, and functions.

6.09 Scope is the boundary of the audit and is directly tied to the audit objectives. The scope defines the subject matter that the auditors will assess and report on, such as a particular program or aspect of a program, the necessary documents or records, the period of time reviewed, and the locations that will be included.

6.10 The methodology describes the nature and extent of audit procedures for gathering and analyzing evidence to address the audit objectives. Audit procedures are the specific steps and tests auditors perform to address the audit objectives. Auditors should design the methodology to obtain reasonable assurance that the evidence is sufficient and appropriate to support the auditors' findings and conclusions in relation to the audit objectives and to reduce audit risk to an acceptable level.

6.11 Auditors should assess audit risk and significance within the context of the audit objectives by gaining an understanding of the following:

a. the nature and profile of the programs and the needs of potential users of the audit report;

b. internal control as it relates to the specific objectives and scope of the audit;

c. information systems controls for purposes of assessing audit risk and planning the audit within the context of the audit objectives;

d. provisions of laws, regulations, contracts, and grant agreements, and potential fraud, and abuse that are significant within the context of the audit objectives;

e. ongoing investigations or legal proceedings within the context of the audit objectives; and

f. the results of previous audits and attestation engagements that directly relate to the current audit objectives.[129]

6.12 During planning, auditors should also

a. identify the potential criteria needed to evaluate matters subject to audit;

b. identify sources of audit evidence and determine the amount and type of evidence needed given audit risk and significance;

c. evaluate whether to use the work of other auditors and specialists to address some of the audit objectives;

d. assign sufficient staff and specialists with adequate collective professional competence and identify other resources needed to perform the audit;

e. communicate about planning and performance of the audit to management officials, those charged with governance, and others as applicable; and

---

[129]See paragraphs 6.13 through 6.36 for additional discussion of 6.11 a-f.

f. prepare a written audit plan.[130]

Nature and Profile of the Program and User Needs

6.13 Auditors should obtain an understanding of the nature of the program or program component under audit and the potential use that will be made of the audit results or report as they plan a performance audit. The nature and profile of a program include

a. visibility, sensitivity, and relevant risks associated with the program under audit;

b. age of the program or changes in its conditions;

c. the size of the program in terms of total dollars, number of citizens affected, or other measures;

d. level and extent of review or other forms of independent oversight;

e. program's strategic plan and objectives; and

f. external factors or conditions that could directly affect the program.

6.14 One group of users of the auditors' report is government officials who may have authorized or requested the audit. Other important users of the auditors' report are the audited entity, those responsible for acting on the auditors' recommendations, oversight organizations, and legislative bodies. Other potential users of the auditors' report include government legislators or officials (other than those who may have authorized or requested the audit), the media, interest groups, and individual citizens. In addition to an interest

---

[130]See paragraphs 6.37 through 6.52 for additional discussion of 6.12 a-f.

in the program, potential users may have an ability to influence the conduct of the program. An awareness of these potential users' interests and influence can help auditors judge whether possible findings could be significant to relevant users.

6.15 Obtaining an understanding of the program under audit helps auditors to assess the relevant risks associated with the program and the impact of the risks on the audit objectives, scope, and methodology. The auditors' understanding may come from knowledge they already have about the program or knowledge they gain from inquiries, observations, and reviewing documents while planning the audit. The extent and breadth of those inquiries and observations will vary among audits based on the audit objectives, as will the need to understand individual aspects of the program, such as the following:

a. Provisions of laws, regulations, contracts and grant agreements: Government programs are usually created by law and are subject to specific laws and regulations. Laws and regulations usually set forth what is to be done, who is to do it, the purpose to be achieved, the population to be served, and related funding guidelines or restrictions. Government programs may also be subject to contracts or grant agreements. Thus, understanding the laws and legislative history establishing a program and the provisions of any contracts or grant agreements is essential to understanding the program itself. Obtaining that understanding is also a necessary step in identifying the provisions of laws, regulations, contracts, or grant agreements that are significant within the context of the audit objectives.

b. Purpose and goals: Purpose is the result or effect that is intended or desired from a program's operation. Legislatures usually establish the program's purpose when they provide authority for the program. Entity officials may provide more detailed information on the program's purpose to supplement the authorizing legislation. Entity officials are sometimes asked to set goals for program performance and operations, including both output and outcome goals. Auditors may use the stated program purpose and goals as criteria for assessing program performance or may develop additional criteria to use when assessing performance.

c. Internal control: Internal control, sometimes referred to as management control, in the broadest sense includes the plan, policies, methods, and procedures adopted by management to meet its missions, goals, and objectives. Internal control includes the processes for planning, organizing, directing, and controlling program operations. It includes the systems for measuring, reporting, and monitoring program performance. Internal control serves as a defense in safeguarding assets and in preventing and detecting errors; fraud; noncompliance with provisions of laws, regulations, contracts or grant agreements; or abuse.[131]

d. Inputs: Inputs are the amount of resources (in terms of money, material, personnel, etc.) that are put into a program. These resources may come from within or outside the entity operating the program. Measures of inputs can have a number of dimensions, such as cost, timing, and quality. Examples of measures of inputs are dollars spent, employee-hours expended, and square feet of building space.

e. Program operations: Program operations are the strategies, processes, and activities management uses

---

[131]See paragraphs 6.16 through 6.27 for guidance pertaining to internal control.

to convert inputs into outputs. Program operations may be subject to internal control.

f. Outputs: Outputs represent the quantity of goods or services produced by a program. For example, an output measure for a job training program could be the number of persons completing training, and an output measure for an aviation safety inspection program could be the number of safety inspections completed.

g. Outcomes: Outcomes are accomplishments or results of a program. For example, an outcome measure for a job training program could be the percentage of trained persons obtaining a job and still in the work place after a specified period of time. An example of an outcome measure for an aviation safety inspection program could be the percentage reduction in safety problems found in subsequent inspections or the percentage of problems deemed corrected in follow-up inspections. Such outcome measures show the progress made in achieving the stated program purpose of helping unemployable citizens obtain and retain jobs, and improving the safety of aviation operations. Outcomes may be influenced by cultural, economic, physical, or technological factors outside the program. Auditors may use approaches drawn from other disciplines, such as program evaluation, to isolate the effects of the program from these other influences. Outcomes also include unexpected and/or unintentional effects of a program, both positive and negative.

Internal Control

6.16 Auditors should obtain an understanding of internal control[132] that is significant within the context of the audit objectives. For internal control that is significant within the context of the audit objectives, auditors should assess whether internal control has been properly designed and implemented and should perform procedures designed to obtain sufficient, appropriate evidence to support their assessment about the effectiveness of those controls. Information systems controls are often an integral part of an entity's internal control. The effectiveness of significant internal controls is frequently dependent on the effectiveness of information systems controls. Thus, when obtaining an understanding of internal control significant to the audit objectives, auditors should also determine whether it is necessary to evaluate information systems controls.[133]

6.17 The effectiveness of internal control that is significant within the context of the audit objectives can affect audit risk. Consequently, auditors may determine that it is necessary to modify the nature, timing, or extent of the audit procedures based on the auditors' assessment of internal control and the results of internal control testing. For example, poorly controlled aspects of a program have a higher risk of failure, so auditors may choose to focus more efforts in these areas. Conversely, effective controls at the audited entity may enable the auditors to limit the extent and type of audit testing needed.

6.18 Auditors may obtain an understanding of internal control through inquiries, observations, inspection of documents and records, review of other auditors'

---

[132]See paragraphs A.03 and A.04 for additional discussion on internal control.

[133]See paragraphs 6.23 through 6.27 for additional discussion on evaluating the effectiveness of information systems controls.

reports, or direct tests. The nature and extent of procedures auditors perform to obtain an understanding of internal control may vary among audits based on audit objectives, audit risk, known or potential internal control deficiencies, and the auditors' knowledge about internal control gained in prior audits.

6.19 The following discussion of the principal types of internal control objectives is intended to help auditors better understand internal controls and determine whether or to what extent they are significant to the audit objectives.

a. Effectiveness and efficiency of program operations: Controls over program operations include policies and procedures that the audited entity has implemented to provide reasonable assurance that a program meets its objectives, while considering cost-effectiveness and efficiency. Understanding these controls can help auditors understand the program operations that convert inputs to outputs and outcomes.

b. Relevance and reliability of information: Controls over the relevance and reliability of information include policies and procedures that officials of the audited entity have implemented to provide themselves reasonable assurance that operational and financial information they use for decision making and reporting externally is relevant and reliable and fairly disclosed in reports. Understanding these controls can help auditors (1) assess the risk that the information gathered by the entity may not be relevant or reliable and (2) design appropriate tests of the information considering the audit objectives.

c. Compliance with applicable laws, regulations, contracts, and grant agreements: Controls over compliance include policies and procedures that the audited entity has implemented to provide reasonable assurance that program implementation is in accordance with provisions of laws, regulations, contracts, and grant agreements. Understanding the relevant controls concerning compliance with those laws, regulations, contracts or grant agreements that the auditors have determined are significant within the context of the audit objectives can help them assess the risk of noncompliance with provisions of laws, regulations, contracts, or grant agreements, or abuse.

6.20 A subset of these categories of internal control objectives is the safeguarding of assets and resources. Controls over the safeguarding of assets and resources include policies and procedures that the audited entity has implemented to reasonably prevent or promptly detect unauthorized acquisition, use, or disposition of assets and resources.

6.21 In performance audits, a deficiency in internal control[134] exists when the design or operation of a control does not allow management or employees, in the normal course of performing their assigned functions, to prevent, or detect and correct (1) impairments of effectiveness or efficiency of operations, (2) misstatements in financial or performance information, or (3) noncompliance with provisions of laws, regulations, contracts, or grant agreements on a timely basis. A deficiency in design exists when (a) a control necessary to meet the control objective is missing or (b) an existing control is not properly designed so that, even if the control operates as designed, the control objective is not met. A deficiency in operation exists when a properly designed control does not operate as designed, or when the person performing the control does not possess the

---

[134]See paragraph A.05 for additional discussion of internal control deficiencies.

necessary authority or qualifications to perform the
control effectively.

6.22 Internal auditing is an important part of overall
governance, accountability, and internal control. A key
role of many internal audit organizations is to provide
assurance that internal controls are in place to
adequately mitigate risks and achieve program goals
and objectives. The auditor may determine that it is
appropriate to use the work of the internal auditors in
the auditor's assessment of the effectiveness of design
or operation of internal controls that are significant
within the context of the audit objectives.[135]

Information Systems Controls

6.23 Understanding information systems controls is
important when information systems are used
extensively throughout the program under audit and the
fundamental business processes related to the audit
objectives rely on information systems. Information
systems controls consist of those internal controls that
are dependent on information systems processing and
include general controls, application controls, and user
controls.

a. Information systems general controls (entitywide,
system, and application levels) are the policies and
procedures that apply to all or a large segment of an
entity's information systems. General controls help
ensure the proper operation of information systems by
creating the environment for proper operation of
application controls. General controls include security
management, logical and physical access, configuration
management, segregation of duties, and contingency
planning.

---

[135]See paragraphs 6.40 through 6.44 for standards and guidance for
using the work of other auditors.

b. Application controls, sometimes referred to as business process controls, are those controls that are incorporated directly into computer applications to help ensure the validity, completeness, accuracy, and confidentiality of transactions and data during application processing. Application controls include controls over input, processing, output, master file, interface, and data management system controls.

c. User controls are portions of controls that are performed by people interacting with information system controls. A user control is an information system control if its effectiveness depends on information systems processing or the reliability (accuracy, completeness, and validity) of information processed by information systems.

6.24 An organization's use of information systems controls may be extensive; however, auditors are primarily interested in those information systems controls that are significant to the audit objectives. Information systems controls are significant to the audit objectives if auditors determine that it is necessary to evaluate the effectiveness of information systems controls in order to obtain sufficient, appropriate evidence. When information systems controls are determined to be significant to the audit objectives or when the effectiveness of significant controls is dependent on the effectiveness of information systems controls, auditors should then evaluate the design and operating effectiveness of such controls. This evaluation would include other information systems controls that impact the effectiveness of the significant controls or the reliability of information used in performing the significant controls. Auditors should obtain a sufficient understanding of information systems

controls necessary to assess audit risk and plan the
audit within the context of the audit objectives.[136]

6.25 Audit procedures to evaluate the effectiveness of
significant information systems controls include
(1) gaining an understanding of the system as it relates
to the information and (2) identifying and evaluating the
general, application, and user controls that are critical to
providing assurance over the reliability of the
information required for the audit.

6.26 The evaluation of information systems controls
may be done in conjunction with the auditors'
consideration of internal control within the context of the
audit objectives[137] or as a separate audit objective or
audit procedure, depending on the objectives of the
audit. Depending on the significance of information
systems controls to the audit objectives, the extent of
audit procedures to obtain such an understanding may
be limited or extensive. In addition, the nature and
extent of audit risk related to information systems
controls are affected by the nature of the hardware and
software used, the configuration of the entity's systems
and networks, and the entity's information systems
strategy.

6.27 Auditors should determine which audit procedures
related to information systems controls are needed to
obtain sufficient, appropriate evidence to support the
audit findings and conclusions. The following factors
may assist auditors in making this determination:

---

[136]Refer to additional criteria and guidance in *Federal Information
System Controls Audit Manual* (FISCAM), GAO-09-232G
(Washington, D.C.: February 2009) and *IT Standards, Guidelines, and
Tools and Techniques for Audit and Assurance and Control
Professionals*, published by ISACA.

[137]See paragraphs 6.16 through 6.22 for additional discussion on
internal control.

a. The extent to which internal controls that are significant to the audit depend on the reliability of information processed or generated by information systems.

b. The availability of evidence outside the information system to support the findings and conclusions: It may not be possible for auditors to obtain sufficient, appropriate evidence without evaluating the effectiveness of relevant information systems controls. For example, if information supporting the findings and conclusions is generated by information systems or its reliability is dependent on information systems controls, there may not be sufficient supporting or corroborating information or documentary evidence that is available other than that produced by the information systems.

c. The relationship of information systems controls to data reliability: To obtain evidence about the reliability of computer-generated information, auditors may decide to evaluate the effectiveness of information systems controls as part of obtaining evidence about the reliability of the data. If the auditor concludes that information systems controls are effective, the auditor may reduce the extent of direct testing of data.

d. Evaluating the effectiveness of information systems controls as an audit objective: When evaluating the effectiveness of information systems controls is directly a part of an audit objective, auditors should test information systems controls necessary to address the audit objectives. For example, the audit may involve the effectiveness of information systems controls related to certain systems, facilities, or organizations.

Provisions of Laws, Regulations, Contracts, and Grant Agreements, Fraud, and Abuse

Provisions of Laws, Regulations, Contracts, and Grant Agreements

6.28 Auditors should identify any provisions of laws, regulations, contracts or grant agreements that are significant within the context of the audit objectives and assess the risk that noncompliance with provisions of laws, regulations, contracts or grant agreements could occur.[138] Based on that risk assessment, the auditors should design and perform procedures to obtain reasonable assurance of detecting instances of noncompliance with provisions of laws, regulations, contracts, or grant agreements that are significant within the context of the audit objectives.

6.29 The auditors' assessment of audit risk may be affected by such factors as the complexity or newness of the laws, regulations, contracts or grant agreements. The auditors' assessment of audit risk also may be affected by whether the entity has controls that are effective in preventing or detecting noncompliance with provisions of laws, regulations, contracts, or grant agreements. If auditors obtain sufficient, appropriate evidence of the effectiveness of these controls, they can reduce the extent of their tests of compliance.

Fraud

6.30 In planning the audit, auditors should assess risks of fraud occurring that is significant within the context of the audit objectives.[139] Fraud involves obtaining something of value through willful misrepresentation.

---

[138]See paragraphs A.11 through A.13 for additional discussion on the significance of provisions of laws, regulations, contracts, or grant agreements.

[139]See paragraph A.10 for examples of indicators of fraud risk.

Whether an act is, in fact, fraud is a determination to be made through the judicial or other adjudicative system and is beyond auditors' professional responsibility. Audit team members should discuss among the team fraud risks, including factors such as individuals' incentives or pressures to commit fraud, the opportunity for fraud to occur, and rationalizations or attitudes that could allow individuals to commit fraud. Auditors should gather and assess information to identify risks of fraud that are significant within the scope of the audit objectives or that could affect the findings and conclusions. For example, auditors may obtain information through discussion with officials of the audited entity or through other means to determine the susceptibility of the program to fraud, the status of internal controls the audited entity has established to prevent and detect fraud, or the risk that officials of the audited entity could override internal control. An attitude of professional skepticism in assessing these risks assists auditors in assessing which factors or risks could significantly affect the audit objectives.

6.31 When auditors identify factors or risks related to fraud that has occurred or is likely to have occurred that they believe are significant within the context of the audit objectives, they should design procedures to obtain reasonable assurance of detecting any such fraud. Assessing the risk of fraud is an ongoing process throughout the audit and relates not only to planning the audit but also to evaluating evidence obtained during the audit.

6.32 When information comes to the auditors' attention indicating that fraud, significant within the context of the audit objectives, may have occurred, auditors should extend the audit steps and procedures, as necessary, to (1) determine whether fraud has likely occurred and (2) if so, determine its effect on the audit findings. If the fraud that may have occurred is not significant within the context of the audit objectives, the auditors may conduct additional audit work as a separate engagement, or refer the matter to other parties with oversight responsibility or jurisdiction.

Abuse

6.33 Abuse involves behavior that is deficient or improper when compared with behavior that a prudent person would consider reasonable and necessary business practice given the facts and circumstances. Abuse also includes misuse of authority or position for personal financial interests or those of an immediate or close family member or business associate.[140] Abuse does not necessarily involve fraud, noncompliance with provisions of laws, regulations, contracts, or grant agreements.

6.34 Because the determination of abuse is subjective, auditors are not required to detect abuse in performance audits. However, as part of a GAGAS audit, if auditors become aware of abuse that could be quantitatively or qualitatively significant to the program under audit, auditors should apply audit procedures specifically directed to ascertain the potential effect on the program under audit within the context of the audit objectives. After performing additional work, auditors may discover that the abuse represents potential fraud or noncompliance with provisions of laws, regulations, contracts, or grant agreements.

Ongoing
Investigations and
Legal Proceedings

6.35 Avoiding interference with investigations or legal proceedings is important in pursuing indications of fraud, noncompliance with provisions of laws, regulations, contracts or grant agreements, or abuse. Laws, regulations, and policies may require auditors to report indications of certain types of fraud, noncompliance with provisions of laws, regulations,

---

[140]See A.08 for additional examples of abuse.

contracts, or grant agreements, or abuse to law enforcement or investigatory authorities before performing additional audit procedures. When investigations or legal proceedings are initiated or in process, auditors should evaluate the impact on the current audit. In some cases, it may be appropriate for the auditors to work with investigators or legal authorities, or withdraw from or defer further work on the audit or a portion of the audit to avoid interfering with an ongoing investigation or legal proceeding.

Previous Audits and Attestation Engagements

6.36 Auditors should evaluate whether the audited entity has taken appropriate corrective action to address findings and recommendations from previous engagements that are significant within the context of the audit objectives. When planning the audit, auditors should ask management of the audited entity to identify previous audits, attestation engagements, performance audits, or other studies that directly relate to the objectives of the audit, including whether related recommendations have been implemented. Auditors should use this information in assessing risk and determining the nature, timing, and extent of current audit work, including determining the extent to which testing the implementation of the corrective actions is applicable to the current audit objectives.

Identifying Audit Criteria

6.37 Auditors should identify criteria. Criteria represent the laws, regulations, contracts, grant agreements, standards, specific requirements, measures, expected performance, defined business practices, and benchmarks against which performance is compared or evaluated. Criteria identify the required or desired state or expectation with respect to the program or operation. Criteria provide a context for evaluating evidence and understanding the findings, conclusions, and recommendations included in the report. Auditors should use criteria that are relevant to the audit

objectives and permit consistent assessment of the
subject matter.[141]

Identifying Sources of Evidence and the Amount and Type of Evidence Required	**6.38** Auditors should identify potential sources of information that could be used as evidence. Auditors should determine the amount and type of evidence needed to obtain sufficient, appropriate evidence to address the audit objectives and adequately plan audit work.
	6.39 If auditors believe that it is likely that sufficient, appropriate evidence will not be available, they may revise the audit objectives or modify the scope and methodology and determine alternative procedures to obtain additional evidence or other forms of evidence to address the current audit objectives. Auditors should also evaluate whether the lack of sufficient, appropriate evidence is due to internal control deficiencies or other program weaknesses, and whether the lack of sufficient, appropriate evidence could be the basis for audit findings.[142]
Using the Work of Others	**6.40** Auditors should determine whether other auditors have conducted, or are conducting, audits of the program that could be relevant to the current audit objectives. The results of other auditors' work may be useful sources of information for planning and performing the audit. If other auditors have identified areas that warrant further audit work or follow-up, their work may influence the auditors' selection of objectives, scope, and methodology.

[141]See paragraph A6.02 for examples of criteria.

[142]See paragraphs 6.56 through 6.72 for standards concerning evidence.

6.41 If other auditors have completed audit work related to the objectives of the current audit, the current auditors may be able to use the work of the other auditors to support findings or conclusions for the current audit and, thereby, avoid duplication of efforts. If auditors use the work of other auditors, they should perform procedures that provide a sufficient basis for using that work. Auditors should obtain evidence concerning the other auditors' qualifications and independence and should determine whether the scope, quality, and timing of the audit work performed by the other auditors is adequate for reliance in the context of the current audit objectives. Procedures that auditors may perform in making this determination include reviewing the other auditors' report, audit plan, or audit documentation, and/or performing tests of the other auditors' work. The nature and extent of evidence needed will depend on the significance of the other auditors' work to the current audit objectives and the extent to which the auditors will use that work.[143]

6.42 Some audits may necessitate the use of specialized techniques or methods that require the skills of a specialist. Specialists to whom this section applies include, but are not limited to, actuaries, appraisers, attorneys, engineers, environmental consultants, medical professionals, statisticians, geologists, and information technology experts. If auditors intend to use the work of specialists, they should assess the professional qualifications and independence of the specialists.

6.43 Auditors' assessment of professional qualifications of the specialist involves the following:

---

[143]See paragraph 3.107 for additional discussion on using the work of other auditors and peer review reports.

a. the professional certification, license, or other recognition of the competence of the specialist in his or her field, as appropriate;

b. the reputation and standing of the specialist in the views of peers and others familiar with the specialist's capability or performance;

c. the specialist's experience and previous work in the subject matter; and

d. the auditors' prior experience in using the specialist's work.

6.44 Auditors' assessment of the independence of specialists who perform audit work includes identifying threats and applying any necessary safeguards in the same manner as they would for auditors performing work on those audits.[144]

Assigning Staff and Other Resources

6.45 Audit management should assign sufficient staff and specialists with adequate collective professional competence to perform the audit.[145] Staffing an audit includes, among other things:

a. assigning staff and specialists with the collective knowledge, skills, and experience appropriate for the job,

b. assigning a sufficient number of staff and supervisors to the audit,

---

[144]See paragraphs 3.02 through 3.26 for additional discussion related to independence and applying the conceptual framework approach to independence.

[145]See paragraphs 3.72 and 3.79 through 3.81 for additional discussion of using specialists in a GAGAS audit.

c. providing for on-the-job training of staff, and

d. engaging specialists when necessary.

6.46 If planning to use the work of a specialist, auditors should document the nature and scope of the work to be performed by the specialist, including

a. the objectives and scope of the specialist's work,

b. the intended use of the specialist's work to support the audit objectives,

c. the specialist's procedures and findings so they can be evaluated and related to other planned audit procedures, and

d. the assumptions and methods used by the specialist.

Communicating with Management, Those Charged with Governance, and Others

6.47 Auditors should communicate an overview of the objectives, scope, and methodology and the timing of the performance audit and planned reporting (including any potential restrictions on the report), unless doing so could significantly impair the auditors' ability to obtain sufficient, appropriate evidence to address the audit objectives, such as when the auditors plan to conduct unannounced cash counts or perform procedures related to indications of fraud. Auditors should communicate with the following parties, as applicable:

a. management of the audited entity, including those with sufficient authority and responsibility to implement corrective action in the program or activity being audited;

b. those charged with governance;[146]

c. the individuals contracting for or requesting audit services, such as contracting officials or grantees; and

d. the cognizant legislative committee, when auditors perform the audit pursuant to a law or regulation or they conduct the work for the legislative committee that has oversight of the audited entity.

6.48 In those situations where there is not a single individual or group that both oversees the strategic direction of the audited entity and the fulfillment of its accountability obligations or in other situations where the identity of those charged with governance is not clearly evident, auditors should document the process followed and conclusions reached for identifying the appropriate individuals to receive the required auditor communications.

6.49 Determining the form, content, and frequency of the communication is a matter of professional judgment, although written communication is preferred. Auditors may use an engagement letter to communicate the information. Auditors should document this communication.

6.50 If an audit is terminated before it is completed and an audit report is not issued, auditors should document the results of the work to the date of termination and why the audit was terminated. Determining whether and how to communicate the reason for terminating the audit to those charged with governance, appropriate officials of the audited entity, the entity contracting for or requesting the audit, and other appropriate officials will

---

[146]See paragraphs A1.05 through A1.07 for a discussion of the role of those charged with governance.

depend on the facts and circumstances and, therefore, is a matter of professional judgment.

Preparing a Written Audit Plan

6.51 Auditors must prepare a written audit plan for each audit. The form and content of the written audit plan may vary among audits and may include an audit strategy, audit program, project plan, audit planning paper, or other appropriate documentation of key decisions about the audit objectives, scope, and methodology and the auditors' basis for those decisions. Auditors should update the plan, as necessary, to reflect any significant changes to the plan made during the audit.

6.52 A written audit plan provides an opportunity for audit organization management to supervise audit planning and to determine whether

a. the proposed audit objectives are likely to result in a useful report;

b. the audit plan adequately addresses relevant risks;

c. the proposed audit scope and methodology are adequate to address the audit objectives;

d. available evidence is likely to be sufficient and appropriate for purposes of the audit; and

e. sufficient staff, supervisors, and specialists with adequate collective professional competence and other resources are available to perform the audit and to meet expected time frames for completing the work.

Supervision

6.53 Audit supervisors or those designated to supervise auditors must properly supervise audit staff.

6.54 Audit supervision involves providing sufficient guidance and direction to staff assigned to the audit to address the audit objectives and follow applicable requirements, while staying informed about significant problems encountered, reviewing the work performed, and providing effective on-the-job training.[147]

6.55 The nature and extent of the supervision of staff and the review of audit work may vary depending on a number of factors, such as the size of the audit organization, the significance of the work, and the experience of the staff.

Obtaining Sufficient, Appropriate Evidence

6.56 Auditors must obtain sufficient, appropriate evidence to provide a reasonable basis for their findings and conclusions.

6.57 The concept of sufficient, appropriate evidence is integral to an audit. Appropriateness is the measure of the quality of evidence that encompasses its relevance, validity, and reliability in providing support for findings and conclusions related to the audit objectives.[148] In assessing the overall appropriateness of evidence, auditors should assess whether the evidence is relevant, valid, and reliable. Sufficiency is a measure of the quantity of evidence used to support the findings and conclusions related to the audit objectives. In assessing the sufficiency of evidence, auditors should determine whether enough evidence has been obtained to persuade a knowledgeable person that the findings are reasonable.

---

[147]See paragraph 6.83c for the documentation requirement related to supervision.

[148]See paragraph A6.05 for additional discussion of the appropriateness of evidence.

6.58 In assessing evidence, auditors should evaluate whether the evidence taken as a whole is sufficient and appropriate for addressing the audit objectives and supporting findings and conclusions. Audit objectives may vary widely, as may the level of work necessary to assess the sufficiency and appropriateness of evidence to address the objectives. For example, in establishing the appropriateness of evidence, auditors may test its reliability by obtaining supporting evidence, using statistical testing, or obtaining corroborating evidence. The concepts of audit risk and significance assist auditors with evaluating the audit evidence.[149]

6.59 Professional judgment assists auditors in determining the sufficiency and appropriateness of evidence taken as a whole. Interpreting, summarizing, or analyzing evidence is typically used in the process of determining the sufficiency and appropriateness of evidence and in reporting the results of the audit work. When appropriate, auditors may use statistical methods to analyze and interpret evidence to assess its sufficiency.

Appropriateness

6.60 Appropriateness is the measure of the quality of evidence that encompasses the relevance, validity, and reliability of evidence used for addressing the audit objectives and supporting findings and conclusions.[150]

a. Relevance refers to the extent to which evidence has a logical relationship with, and importance to, the issue being addressed.

---

[149]See paragraphs 6.04 and 6.05 for a discussion of significance and audit risk.

[150]See paragraph A6.05 for additional guidance regarding assessing the appropriateness of evidence in relation to the audit objectives.

b. Validity refers to the extent to which evidence is a meaningful or reasonable basis for measuring what is being evaluated. In other words, validity refers to the extent to which evidence represents what it is purported to represent.

c. Reliability refers to the consistency of results when information is measured or tested and includes the concepts of being verifiable or supported.[151]

6.61 There are different types and sources of evidence that auditors may use, depending on the audit objectives. Evidence may be obtained by observation, inquiry, or inspection. Each type of evidence has its own strengths and weaknesses.[152] The following contrasts are useful in judging the appropriateness of evidence. However, these contrasts are not adequate in themselves to determine appropriateness. The nature and types of evidence to support auditors' findings and conclusions are matters of the auditors' professional judgment based on the audit objectives and audit risk.

a. Evidence obtained when internal control is effective is generally more reliable than evidence obtained when internal control is weak or nonexistent.

b. Evidence obtained through the auditors' direct physical examination, observation, computation, and inspection is generally more reliable than evidence obtained indirectly.

c. Examination of original documents is generally more reliable than examination of copies.

---

[151]See paragraph 6.66 for a discussion of computer-processed information and guidance on data reliability.

[152]See paragraph A6.04 for additional guidance regarding the types of evidence.

d. Testimonial evidence obtained under conditions in which persons may speak freely is generally more reliable than evidence obtained under circumstances in which the persons may be intimidated.

e. Testimonial evidence obtained from an individual who is not biased and has direct knowledge about the area is generally more reliable than testimonial evidence obtained from an individual who is biased or has indirect or partial knowledge about the area.

f. Evidence obtained from a knowledgeable, credible, and unbiased third party is generally more reliable than evidence obtained from management of the audited entity or others who have a direct interest in the audited entity.

6.62 Testimonial evidence may be useful in interpreting or corroborating documentary or physical information. Auditors should evaluate the objectivity, credibility, and reliability of the testimonial evidence. Documentary evidence may be used to help verify, support, or challenge testimonial evidence.

6.63 Surveys generally provide self-reported information about existing conditions or programs. Evaluation of the survey design and administration assists auditors in evaluating the objectivity, credibility, and reliability of the self-reported information.

6.64 When sampling is used, the method of selection that is appropriate will depend on the audit objectives. When a representative sample is needed, the use of statistical sampling approaches generally results in stronger evidence than that obtained from nonstatistical techniques. When a representative sample is not needed, a targeted selection may be effective if the auditors have isolated risk factors or other criteria to target the selection.

6.65 When auditors use information provided by officials of the audited entity as part of their evidence, they should determine what the officials of the audited entity or other auditors did to obtain assurance over the reliability of the information. The auditor may find it necessary to perform testing of management's procedures to obtain assurance or perform direct testing of the information. The nature and extent of the auditors' procedures will depend on the significance of the information to the audit objectives and the nature of the information being used.

6.66 Auditors should assess the sufficiency and appropriateness of computer-processed information regardless of whether this information is provided to auditors or auditors independently extract it. The nature, timing, and extent of audit procedures to assess sufficiency and appropriateness is affected by the effectiveness of the audited entity's internal controls over the information, including information systems controls, and the significance of the information and the level of detail presented in the auditors' findings and conclusions in light of the audit objectives.[153] The assessment of the sufficiency and appropriateness of computer-processed information includes considerations regarding the completeness and accuracy of the data for the intended purposes.[154]

Sufficiency

6.67 Sufficiency is a measure of the quantity of evidence used for addressing the audit objectives and supporting findings and conclusions. Sufficiency also depends on the appropriateness of the evidence. In

---

[153]See paragraphs 6.23 through 6.27 for additional discussion on assessing the effectiveness of information systems controls.

[154]Refer to additional guidance in *Assessing the Reliability of Computer-Processed Data*, GAO-09-680G (Washington, D.C.: July 2009).

determining the sufficiency of evidence, auditors should
determine whether enough appropriate evidence exists
to address the audit objectives and support the findings
and conclusions.

6.68 The following presumptions are useful in judging
the sufficiency of evidence. The sufficiency of evidence
required to support the auditors' findings and
conclusions is a matter of the auditors' professional
judgment.

a. The greater the audit risk, the greater the quantity
and quality of evidence required.

b. Stronger evidence may allow less evidence to be
used.

c. Having a large volume of audit evidence does not
compensate for a lack of relevance, validity, or
reliability.

Overall Assessment of Evidence

6.69 Auditors should determine the overall sufficiency
and appropriateness of evidence to provide a
reasonable basis for the findings and conclusions,
within the context of the audit objectives. Professional
judgments about the sufficiency and appropriateness of
evidence are closely interrelated, as auditors interpret
the results of audit testing and evaluate whether the
nature and extent of the evidence obtained is sufficient
and appropriate. Auditors should perform and
document an overall assessment of the collective
evidence used to support findings and conclusions,
including the results of any specific assessments
conducted to conclude on the validity and reliability of
specific evidence.

6.70 Sufficiency and appropriateness of evidence are
relative concepts, which may be thought of in terms of a

continuum rather than as absolutes. Sufficiency and appropriateness are evaluated in the context of the related findings and conclusions. For example, even though the auditors may have some limitations or uncertainties about the sufficiency or appropriateness of some of the evidence, they may nonetheless determine that in total there is sufficient, appropriate evidence to support the findings and conclusions.

6.71 When assessing the sufficiency and appropriateness of evidence, auditors should evaluate the expected significance of evidence to the audit objectives, findings, and conclusions, available corroborating evidence, and the level of audit risk. The steps to assess evidence may depend on the nature of the evidence, how the evidence is used in the audit or report, and the audit objectives.

a. Evidence is sufficient and appropriate when it provides a reasonable basis for supporting the findings or conclusions within the context of the audit objectives.

b. Evidence is not sufficient or not appropriate when (1) using the evidence carries an unacceptably high risk that it could lead the auditor to reach an incorrect or improper conclusion, (2) the evidence has significant limitations, given the audit objectives and intended use of the evidence, or (3) the evidence does not provide an adequate basis for addressing the audit objectives or supporting the findings and conclusions. Auditors should not use such evidence as support for findings and conclusions.

6.72 Evidence has limitations or uncertainties when the validity or reliability of the evidence has not been assessed or cannot be assessed, given the audit objectives and the intended use of the evidence. Limitations also include errors identified by the auditors in their testing. When the auditors identify limitations or uncertainties in evidence that is significant to the audit findings and conclusions, they should apply additional procedures, as appropriate. Such procedures include

a. seeking independent, corroborating evidence from other sources;

b. redefining the audit objectives or limiting the audit scope to eliminate the need to use the evidence;

c. presenting the findings and conclusions so that the supporting evidence is sufficient and appropriate and describing in the report the limitations or uncertainties with the validity or reliability of the evidence, if such disclosure is necessary to avoid misleading the report users about the findings or conclusions;[155] and

d. determining whether to report the limitations or uncertainties as a finding, including any related, significant internal control deficiencies.

Developing Elements of a Finding

6.73 Auditors should plan and perform procedures to develop the elements of a finding necessary to address the audit objectives.[156] In addition, if auditors are able to sufficiently develop the elements of a finding, they should develop recommendations for corrective action if they are significant within the context of the audit objectives. The elements needed for a finding are related to the objectives of the audit. Thus, a finding or set of findings is complete to the extent that the audit objectives are addressed and the report clearly relates those objectives to the elements of a finding. For

---

[155]See paragraph 7.15 for additional reporting requirements when there are limitations or uncertainties with the validity or reliability of evidence.

[156]See paragraph A6.06 for additional discussion on findings.

example, an audit objective may be to determine the current status or condition of program operations or progress in implementing legislative requirements, and not the related cause or effect. In this situation, developing the condition would address the audit objective and development of the other elements of a finding would not be necessary.

6.74 The element of criteria is discussed in paragraph 6.37, and the other elements of a finding—condition, effect, and cause—are discussed in paragraphs 6.75 through 6.77.

6.75 Condition: Condition is a situation that exists. The condition is determined and documented during the audit.

6.76 Cause: The cause identifies the reason or explanation for the condition or the factor or factors responsible for the difference between the situation that exists (condition) and the required or desired state (criteria), which may also serve as a basis for recommendations for corrective actions. Common factors include poorly designed policies, procedures, or criteria; inconsistent, incomplete, or incorrect implementation; or factors beyond the control of program management. Auditors may assess whether the evidence provides a reasonable and convincing argument for why the stated cause is the key factor or factors contributing to the difference between the condition and the criteria.[157]

6.77 Effect or potential effect: The effect is a clear, logical link to establish the impact or potential impact of the difference between the situation that exists (condition) and the required or desired state (criteria).

---

[157]See paragraph A6.06 for additional discussion on cause.

The effect or potential effect identifies the outcomes or consequences of the condition. When the audit objectives include identifying the actual or potential consequences of a condition that varies (either positively or negatively) from the criteria identified in the audit, "effect" is a measure of those consequences. Effect or potential effect may be used to demonstrate the need for corrective action in response to identified problems or relevant risks.[158]

Early Communication of Deficiencies

6.78 Auditors report deficiencies in internal control, fraud, noncompliance with provisions of laws, regulations, contracts, or grant agreements, or abuse. For some matters, early communication to those charged with governance or management may be important because of their relative significance and the urgency for corrective follow-up action. Further, when a control deficiency results in noncompliance with provisions of laws, regulations, contracts or grant agreements, or abuse, early communication is important to allow management to take prompt corrective action to prevent further noncompliance. When a deficiency is communicated early, the reporting requirements in paragraphs 7.18 through 7.23 still apply.

Audit Documentation

6.79 Auditors must prepare audit documentation related to planning, conducting, and reporting for each audit. Auditors should prepare audit documentation in sufficient detail to enable an experienced auditor, having no previous connection to the audit, to understand from the audit documentation the nature, timing, extent, and results of audit procedures performed, the audit evidence obtained and its source

---

[158]See paragraph A6.07 for additional discussion on effect.

and the conclusions reached, including evidence that supports the auditors' significant judgments and conclusions. An experienced auditor means an individual (whether internal or external to the audit organization) who possesses the competencies and skills that would have enabled him or her to conduct the performance audit. These competencies and skills include an understanding of (1) the performance audit processes, (2) GAGAS and applicable legal and regulatory requirements, (3) the subject matter associated with achieving the audit objectives, and (4) issues related to the audited entity's environment.

6.80 Auditors should prepare audit documentation that contains evidence that supports the findings, conclusions, and recommendations before they issue their report.

6.81 Auditors should design the form and content of audit documentation to meet the circumstances of the particular audit. The audit documentation constitutes the principal record of the work that the auditors have performed in accordance with standards and the conclusions that the auditors have reached. The quantity, type, and content of audit documentation are a matter of the auditors' professional judgment.

6.82 Audit documentation is an essential element of audit quality. The process of preparing and reviewing audit documentation contributes to the quality of an audit. Audit documentation serves to (1) provide the principal support for the auditors' report, (2) aid auditors in conducting and supervising the audit, and (3) allow for the review of audit quality.

6.83 Auditors should document[159] the following:

a. the objectives, scope, and methodology of the audit;

b. the work performed and evidence obtained to support significant judgments and conclusions, including descriptions of transactions and records examined (for example, by listing file numbers, case numbers, or other means of identifying specific documents examined, but copies of documents examined or detailed listings of information from those documents are not required); and

c. supervisory review, before the audit report is issued, of the evidence that supports the findings, conclusions, and recommendations contained in the audit report.

6.84 When auditors do not comply with applicable GAGAS requirements due to law, regulation, scope limitations, restrictions on access to records, or other issues impacting the audit, the auditors should document the departure from the GAGAS requirements and the impact on the audit and on the auditors' conclusions. This applies to departures from unconditional requirements and from presumptively mandatory requirements when alternative procedures performed in the circumstances were not sufficient to achieve the objectives of the standard.[160]

6.85 Underlying GAGAS audits is the premise that audit organizations in federal, state, and local governments and public accounting firms engaged to perform audits in accordance with GAGAS cooperate in auditing

---

[159]See paragraphs 6.06, 6.46, 6.48, 6.49, 6.50, 6.69, 6.84, 7.19, 7.22, and 7.44 for additional documentation requirements regarding performance audits.

[160]See paragraphs 2.24 and 2.25 for additional requirements on citing compliance with GAGAS.

programs of common interest so that auditors may use others' work and avoid duplication of efforts. Subject to applicable laws and regulations, auditors should make appropriate individuals, as well as audit documentation, available upon request and in a timely manner to other auditors or reviewers to satisfy these objectives. The use of auditors' work by other auditors may be facilitated by contractual arrangements for GAGAS audits that provide for full and timely access to appropriate individuals, as well as audit documentation.

Chapter 7

Reporting Standards for Performance Audits

| Introduction | **7.01** This chapter contains reporting requirements and guidance for performance audits conducted in accordance with generally accepted government auditing standards (GAGAS). The purpose of reporting requirements is to establish the overall approach for auditors to apply in communicating the results of the performance audit. The reporting requirements for performance audits relate to the form of the report, the report contents, and report issuance and distribution.[161] |

7.02 For performance audits conducted in accordance with GAGAS, the requirements and guidance in chapters 1 through 3, 6, and 7 apply.

| Reporting | **7.03** Auditors must issue audit reports communicating the results of each completed performance audit. |

7.04 Auditors should use a form of the audit report that is appropriate for its intended use and is in writing or in some other retrievable form.[162] For example, auditors may present audit reports using electronic media that are retrievable by report users and the audit organization. The users' needs will influence the form of the audit report. Different forms of audit reports include written reports, letters, briefing slides, or other presentation materials.

---

[161]See paragraph A7.02 for a description of report quality elements.

[162]See paragraph 7.43 for situations when audit organizations are subject to public records laws.

7.05 The purposes of audit reports are to
(1) communicate the results of audits to those charged
with governance, the appropriate officials of the audited
entity, and the appropriate oversight officials; (2) make
the results less susceptible to misunderstanding;
(3) make the results available to the public, unless
specifically limited;[163] and (4) facilitate follow-up to
determine whether appropriate corrective actions have
been taken.

7.06 If an audit is terminated before it is completed and
an audit report is not issued, auditors should follow the
guidance in paragraph 6.50.

7.07 If, after the report is issued, the auditors discover
that they did not have sufficient, appropriate evidence to
support the reported findings or conclusions, they
should communicate in the same manner as that used
to originally distribute the report to those charged with
governance, the appropriate officials of the audited
entity, the appropriate officials of the organizations
requiring or arranging for the audits, and other known
users, so that they do not continue to rely on the
findings or conclusions that were not supported. If the
report was previously posted to the auditors' publicly
accessible website, the auditors should remove the
report and post a public notification that the report was
removed. The auditors should then determine whether
to conduct additional audit work necessary to reissue
the report, including any revised findings or conclusions
or repost the original report if the additional audit work
does not result in a change in findings or conclusions.

---

[163]See paragraph 7.40 for additional guidance on classified or limited
use reports and paragraph 7.44b for distr bution of reports for internal
auditors.

Report Contents

7.08 Auditors should prepare audit reports that contain (1) the objectives, scope, and methodology of the audit; (2) the audit results, including findings, conclusions, and recommendations, as appropriate; (3) a statement about the auditors' compliance with GAGAS; (4) a summary of the views of responsible officials; and (5) if applicable, the nature of any confidential or sensitive information omitted.

Objectives, Scope, and Methodology

7.09 Auditors should include in the report a description of the audit objectives and the scope and methodology used for addressing the audit objectives. Report users need this information to understand the purpose of the audit, the nature and extent of the audit work performed, the context and perspective regarding what is reported, and any significant limitations in audit objectives, scope, or methodology.

7.10 Audit objectives for performance audits may vary widely. Auditors should communicate audit objectives in the audit report in a clear, specific, neutral, and unbiased manner that includes relevant assumptions. When audit objectives are limited but broader objectives could be inferred by users, auditors should state in the audit report that certain issues were outside the scope of the audit in order to avoid potential misunderstanding.

7.11 Auditors should describe the scope of the work performed and any limitations, including issues that would be relevant to likely users, so that they could reasonably interpret the findings, conclusions, and recommendations in the report without being misled. Auditors should also report any significant constraints imposed on the audit approach by information limitations or scope impairments, including denials or excessive delays of access to certain records or individuals.

7.12 In describing the work conducted to address the audit objectives and support the reported findings and conclusions, auditors should, as applicable, explain the relationship between the population and the items tested; identify organizations, geographic locations, and the period covered; report the kinds and sources of evidence; and explain any significant limitations or uncertainties based on the auditors' overall assessment of the sufficiency and appropriateness of the evidence in the aggregate.

7.13 In reporting audit methodology, auditors should explain how the completed audit work supports the audit objectives, including the evidence gathering and analysis techniques, in sufficient detail to allow knowledgeable users of their reports to understand how the auditors addressed the audit objectives. Auditors may include a description of the procedures performed as part of their assessment of the sufficiency and appropriateness of information used as audit evidence. Auditors should identify significant assumptions made in conducting the audit; describe comparative techniques applied; describe the criteria used; and, when sampling significantly supports the auditors' findings, conclusions, or recommendations, describe the sample design and state why the design was chosen, including whether the results can be projected to the intended population.

Reporting Findings

7.14 In the audit report, auditors should present sufficient, appropriate evidence to support the findings and conclusions in relation to the audit objectives. Clearly developed findings[164] assist management and oversight officials of the audited entity in understanding the need for taking corrective action. If auditors are able

---

[164]See paragraphs 6.73 through 6.77 for additional discussion on developing the elements of a finding.

to sufficiently develop the elements of a finding, they
should provide recommendations for corrective action if
they are significant within the context of the audit
objectives. However, the extent to which the elements
for a finding are developed depends on the audit
objectives. Thus, a finding or set of findings is complete
to the extent that the auditors address the audit
objectives.

7.15 Auditors should describe in their report limitations
or uncertainties with the reliability or validity of evidence
if (1) the evidence is significant to the findings and
conclusions within the context of the audit objectives
and (2) such disclosure is necessary to avoid
misleading the report users about the findings and
conclusions. As discussed in paragraphs 6.69 through
6.72, even though the auditors may have some
uncertainty about the sufficiency or appropriateness of
some of the evidence, they may nonetheless determine
that in total there is sufficient, appropriate evidence
given the findings and conclusions. Auditors should
describe the limitations or uncertainties regarding
evidence in conjunction with the findings and
conclusions, in addition to describing those limitations
or uncertainties as part of the objectives, scope, and
methodology. Additionally, this description provides
report users with a clear understanding regarding how
much responsibility the auditors are taking for the
information.

7.16 Auditors should place their findings in perspective
by describing the nature and extent of the issues being
reported and the extent of the work performed that
resulted in the finding. To give the reader a basis for
judging the prevalence and consequences of these
findings, auditors should, as appropriate, relate the
instances identified to the population or the number of
cases examined and quantify the results in terms of
dollar value, or other measures. If the results cannot be

projected, auditors should limit their conclusions appropriately.

7.17 Auditors may provide background information to establish the context for the overall message and to help the reader understand the findings and significance of the issues discussed. Appropriate background information may include information on how programs and operations work; the significance of programs and operations (e.g., dollars, impact, purposes, and past audit work, if relevant); a description of the audited entity's responsibilities; and explanation of terms, organizational structure, and the statutory basis for the program and operations. When reporting on the results of their work, auditors should disclose significant facts relevant to the objectives of their work and known to them which, if not disclosed, could mislead knowledgeable users, misrepresent the results, or conceal significant improper or illegal practices.

7.18 Auditors should also report deficiencies in internal control, instances of fraud, noncompliance with provisions of laws, regulations, contracts, or grant agreements, or abuse that have occurred or are likely to have occurred and are significant within the context of the audit objectives.

Deficiencies in Internal Control

7.19 Auditors should include in the audit report (1) the scope of their work on internal control and (2) any deficiencies in internal control that are significant within the context of the audit objectives and based upon the audit work performed.[165] When auditors detect deficiencies in internal control that are not significant to the objectives of the audit but warrant the attention of those charged with governance, they should include

---

[165]See paragraph 6.21 for a discussion of internal control deficiencies in performance audits and paragraph A.06 for examples of deficiencies in internal control.

those deficiencies either in the report or communicate those deficiencies in writing to audited entity officials. Auditors should refer to that written communication in the audit report if the written communication is separate from the audit report. When auditors detect deficiencies that do not warrant the attention of those charged with governance, the determination of whether and how to communicate such deficiencies to audited entity officials is a matter of professional judgment.

7.20 In a performance audit, auditors may conclude that identified deficiencies in internal control that are significant within the context of the audit objectives are the cause of deficient performance of the program or operations being audited. In reporting this type of finding, the internal control deficiency would be described as the cause.

Fraud, Noncompliance with Provisions of Laws, Regulations, Contracts, and Grant Agreements, and Abuse

7.21 When auditors conclude, based on sufficient, appropriate evidence, that fraud,[166] noncompliance with provisions of laws, regulations, contracts or grant agreements, or abuse[167] either has occurred or is likely to have occurred which is significant within the context of the audit objectives, they should report the matter as a finding. Whether a particular act is, in fact, fraud or noncompliance with provisions of laws, regulations, contracts or grant agreements may have to await final determination by a court of law or other adjudicative body.

7.22 When auditors detect instances of fraud, noncompliance with provisions of laws, regulations, contracts, or grant agreements, or abuse that are not significant within the context of the audit objectives but warrant the attention of those charged with governance,

---

[166]See paragraph A.10 for examples of indicators of fraud risk.

[167]See paragraph A.08 for examples of abuse.

they should communicate those findings in writing to audited entity officials. When auditors detect any instances of fraud, noncompliance with provisions of laws, regulations, contracts, or grant agreements, or abuse that do not warrant the attention of those charged with governance, the auditors' determination of whether and how to communicate such instances to audited entity officials is a matter of professional judgment.

7.23 When fraud, noncompliance with provisions of laws, regulations, contracts, or grant agreements, or abuse either have occurred or are likely to have occurred, auditors may consult with authorities or legal counsel about whether publicly reporting such information would compromise investigative or legal proceedings. Auditors may limit their public reporting to matters that would not compromise those proceedings and, for example, report only on information that is already a part of the public record.

Reporting Findings Directly to Parties Outside the Audited Entity

7.24 Auditors should report known or likely fraud, noncompliance with provisions of laws, regulations, contracts, or grant agreements, or abuse directly to parties outside the audited entity in the following two circumstances.

a. When entity management fails to satisfy legal or regulatory requirements to report such information to external parties specified in law or regulation, auditors should first communicate the failure to report such information to those charged with governance. If the audited entity still does not report this information to the specified external parties as soon as practicable after the auditors' communication with those charged with governance, then the auditors should report the information directly to the specified external parties.

b. When entity management fails to take timely and appropriate steps to respond to known or likely fraud, noncompliance with provisions of laws, regulations, contracts, or grant agreements, or abuse that (1) is significant to the findings and conclusions and (2) involves funding received directly or indirectly from a government agency, auditors should first report management's failure to take timely and appropriate steps to those charged with governance. If the audited entity still does not take timely and appropriate steps as soon as practicable after the auditors' communication with those charged with governance, then the auditors should report the entity's failure to take timely and appropriate steps directly to the funding agency.

7.25 The reporting in paragraph 7.24 is in addition to any legal requirements for the auditor to report such information directly to parties outside the audited entity. Auditors should comply with these requirements even if they have resigned or been dismissed from the audit prior to its completion. Internal audit organizations do not have a duty to report outside the audited entity unless required by law, rule, regulation, or policy.[168]

7.26 Auditors should obtain sufficient, appropriate evidence, such as confirmation from outside parties, to corroborate assertions by management of the audited entity that it has reported such findings in accordance with laws, regulations, or funding agreements. When auditors are unable to do so, they should report such information directly as discussed in paragraphs 7.24 and 7.25.

Conclusions

7.27 Auditors should report conclusions based on the audit objectives and the audit findings. Report conclusions are logical inferences about the program based on the auditors' findings, not merely a summary

---

[168]See paragraph 7.44b for reporting standards for internal audit organizations when reporting externally.

of the findings. The strength of the auditors' conclusions depends on the sufficiency and appropriateness of the evidence supporting the findings and the soundness of the logic used to formulate the conclusions. Conclusions are more compelling if they lead to the auditors' recommendations and convince the knowledgeable user of the report that action is necessary.

Recommendations

7.28 Auditors should recommend actions to correct deficiencies and other findings identified during the audit and to improve programs and operations when the potential for improvement in programs, operations, and performance is substantiated by the reported findings and conclusions. Auditors should make recommendations that flow logically from the findings and conclusions, are directed at resolving the cause of identified deficiencies and findings, and clearly state the actions recommended.

7.29 Effective recommendations encourage improvements in the conduct of government programs and operations. Recommendations are effective when they are addressed to parties that have the authority to act and when the recommended actions are specific, practical, cost effective, and measurable.

Reporting Auditors' Compliance with GAGAS

7.30 When auditors comply with all applicable GAGAS requirements, they should use the following language, which represents an unmodified GAGAS compliance statement, in the audit report to indicate that they performed the audit in accordance with GAGAS.[169]

---

[169]See paragraphs 2.24 and 2.25 for additional standards on citing compliance with GAGAS.

We conducted this performance audit in accordance with generally accepted government auditing standards. Those standards require that we plan and perform the audit to obtain sufficient, appropriate evidence to provide a reasonable basis for our findings and conclusions based on our audit objectives. We believe that the evidence obtained provides a reasonable basis for our findings and conclusions based on our audit objectives.

7.31 When auditors do not comply with all applicable GAGAS requirements, they should include a modified GAGAS compliance statement in the audit report. For performance audits, auditors should use a statement that includes either (1) the language in 7.30, modified to indicate the requirements that were not followed or (2) language that the auditor did not follow GAGAS.[170]

Reporting Views of Responsible Officials

7.32 Auditors should obtain and report the views of responsible officials of the audited entity concerning the findings, conclusions, and recommendations included in the audit report, as well as any planned corrective actions.

7.33 Providing a draft report with findings for review and comment by responsible officials of the audited entity and others helps the auditors develop a report that is fair, complete, and objective. Including the views of responsible officials results in a report that presents not only the auditors' findings, conclusions, and recommendations, but also the perspectives of the responsible officials of the audited entity and the corrective actions they plan to take. Obtaining the comments in writing is preferred, but oral comments are acceptable.

---

[170]See paragraphs 2.24 and 2.25 for additional standards on citing compliance with GAGAS.

7.34 When auditors receive written comments from the responsible officials, they should include in their report a copy of the officials' written comments, or a summary of the comments received. When the responsible officials provide oral comments only, auditors should prepare a summary of the oral comments and provide a copy of the summary to the responsible officials to verify that the comments are accurately stated.

7.35 Auditors should also include in the report an evaluation of the comments, as appropriate. In cases in which the audited entity provides technical comments in addition to its written or oral comments on the report, auditors may disclose in the report that such comments were received.

7.36 Obtaining oral comments may be appropriate when, for example, there is a reporting date critical to meeting a user's needs; auditors have worked closely with the responsible officials throughout the work and the parties are familiar with the findings and issues addressed in the draft report; or the auditors do not expect major disagreements with the findings, conclusions, and recommendations in the draft, or major controversies with regard to the issues discussed in the draft report.

7.37 When the audited entity's comments are inconsistent or in conflict with the findings, conclusions, or recommendations in the draft report, or when planned corrective actions do not adequately address the auditors' recommendations, the auditors should evaluate the validity of the audited entity's comments. If the auditors disagree with the comments, they should explain in the report their reasons for disagreement. Conversely, the auditors should modify their report as necessary if they find the comments valid and supported with sufficient, appropriate evidence.

7.38 If the audited entity refuses to provide comments or is unable to provide comments within a reasonable period of time, the auditors may issue the report without receiving comments from the audited entity. In such cases, the auditors should indicate in the report that the audited entity did not provide comments.

Reporting Confidential and Sensitive Information

7.39 If certain pertinent information is prohibited from public disclosure or is excluded from a report due to the confidential or sensitive nature of the information, auditors should disclose in the report that certain information has been omitted and the reason or other circumstances that make the omission necessary.

7.40 Certain information may be classified or may be otherwise prohibited from general disclosure by federal, state, or local laws or regulations. In such circumstances, auditors may issue a separate, classified or limited use report containing such information and distribute the report only to persons authorized by law or regulation to receive it.

7.41 Additional circumstances associated with public safety, privacy, or security concerns could also justify the exclusion of certain information from a publicly available or widely distributed report. For example, detailed information related to computer security for a particular program may be excluded from publicly available reports because of the potential damage that could be caused by the misuse of this information. In such circumstances, auditors may issue a limited use report containing such information and distribute the report only to those parties responsible for acting on the auditors' recommendations. In some instances, it may be appropriate to issue both a publicly available report with the sensitive information excluded and a limited use report. The auditors may consult with legal counsel regarding any requirements or other circumstances that may necessitate the omission of certain information.

7.42 Considering the broad public interest in the program or activity under audit assists auditors when deciding whether to exclude certain information from publicly available reports. When circumstances call for omission of certain information, auditors should evaluate whether this omission could distort the audit results or conceal improper or illegal practices.

7.43 When audit organizations are subject to public records laws, auditors should determine whether public records laws could impact the availability of classified or limited use reports and determine whether other means of communicating with management and those charged with governance would be more appropriate. For example, the auditors may communicate general information in a written report and communicate detailed information orally. The auditor may consult with legal counsel regarding applicable public records laws.

Distributing Reports

7.44 Distribution of reports completed in accordance with GAGAS depends on the relationship of the auditors to the audited organization and the nature of the information contained in the report. Auditors should document any limitation on report distribution.[171] The following discussion outlines distribution for reports completed in accordance with GAGAS:

a. Audit organizations in government entities should distribute audit reports to those charged with governance, to the appropriate audited entity officials, and to the appropriate oversight bodies or organizations requiring or arranging for the audits. As appropriate, auditors should also distribute copies of the reports to other officials who have legal oversight authority or who

---

[171]See paragraphs 7.40 and 7.41 for discussion of limited use reports containing confidential or sensitive information.

may be responsible for acting on audit findings and recommendations, and to others authorized to receive such reports.

b. Internal audit organizations in government entities may also follow the Institute of Internal Auditors' (IIA) *International Standards for the Professional Practice of Internal Auditing.*[172] In accordance with GAGAS and IIA standards, the head of the internal audit organization should communicate results to parties who can ensure that the results are given due consideration. If not otherwise mandated by statutory or regulatory requirements, prior to releasing results to parties outside the organization, the head of the internal audit organization should: (1) assess the potential risk to the organization, (2) consult with senior management or legal counsel as appropriate, and (3) control dissemination by indicating the intended users of the report.

c. Public accounting firms contracted to perform an audit in accordance with GAGAS should clarify report distribution responsibilities with the engaging organization. If the contracting firm is responsible for the distribution, It should reach agreement with the party contracting for the audit about which officials or organizations will receive the report and the steps being taken to make the report available to the public.

---

[172]See paragraph 2.21 for additional discussion about using the IIA standards in conjunction with GAGAS and paragraph 2.22 for additional discussion about citing compliance with another set of standards.

Supplemental Guidance

Introduction

A.01 The following sections provide supplemental guidance for auditors and the audited entities to assist in the implementation of generally accepted government auditing standards (GAGAS). The guidance does not establish additional requirements but instead is intended to facilitate auditor implementation of GAGAS requirements in chapters 2 through 7. The supplemental guidance in the first section may be of assistance for all types of audits covered by GAGAS. Subsequent sections provide supplemental guidance for specific chapters of GAGAS, as indicated.

Overall Supplemental Guidance

A.02 Chapters 4 through 7 discuss the standards for financial audits, attestation engagements, and performance audits. The identification and communication of significant deficiencies and material weaknesses in internal control, fraud, noncompliance with provisions of laws, regulations, contracts or grant agreements, or abuse are important aspects of government auditing. The following discussion is provided to assist auditors in identifying significant deficiencies in internal control, abuse, and indicators of fraud risk and to assist auditors in determining whether noncompliance with provisions of laws, regulations, contracts or grant agreements are significant within the context of the audit objectives.

Internal Control

A.03 The *Internal Control—Integrated Framework*[173] published by the Committee of Sponsoring Organizations of the Treadway Commission (COSO) provides guidance on internal control. As discussed in the COSO framework, internal control consists of five interrelated components, which are (1) control

---

[173]*Internal Control—Integrated Framework*, Committee of Sponsoring Organizations of the Treadway Commission, 1992.

environment, (2) risk assessment, (3) control activities, (4) information and communication, and (5) monitoring. The objectives of internal control relate to (1) financial reporting, (2) operations, and (3) compliance. Safeguarding of assets is a subset of these objectives. Management designs internal control to provide reasonable assurance that unauthorized acquisition, use, or disposition of assets will be prevented or timely detected and corrected.

A.04 In addition to the COSO framework, the publication, *Standards for Internal Control in the Federal Government*,[174] which incorporates the concepts developed by COSO, provides definitions and fundamental concepts pertaining to internal control at the federal level and may also be useful to auditors at other levels of government. The related *Internal Control Management and Evaluation Tool*,[175] based on the federal internal control standards, provides a systematic, organized, and structured approach to assessing the internal control structure.

Examples of Deficiencies in Internal Control

A.05 GAGAS contains requirements for reporting identified deficiencies in internal control.

a. For financial audits, see paragraphs 4.19 through 4.24.

b. For attestation engagements, see paragraphs 5.20 through 5.23.

---

[174]*Standards for Internal Control in the Federal Government*, GAO/AIMD-00-21.3.1 (Washington, D.C.: November 1999).

[175]*Internal Control Management and Evaluation Tool*, GAO-01-1008G (Washington, D.C.: August 2001).

c. For performance audits, see paragraphs 7.19 through 7.20.

A.06 The following are examples of control deficiencies:

a. Insufficient control consciousness within the organization. For example, the tone at the top and the control environment. Control deficiencies in other components of internal control could lead the auditor to conclude that weaknesses exist in the control environment.

b. Ineffective oversight by those charged with governance of the entity's financial reporting, performance reporting, or internal control, or an ineffective overall governance structure.

c. Control systems that did not prevent, or detect and correct material misstatements so that it was necessary to restate previously issued financial statements or operational results. Control systems that did not prevent or detect material misstatements in performance or operational results so that it was later necessary to make significant corrections to those results.

d. Control systems that did not prevent, or detect and correct material misstatements identified by the auditor. This includes misstatements involving estimation and judgment for which the auditor identifies potential material adjustments and corrections of the recorded amounts.

e. An ineffective internal audit function or risk assessment function at an entity for which such functions are important to the monitoring or risk assessment component of internal control, such as for a large or complex entity.

f. Identification of fraud of any magnitude on the part of senior management.

g. Failure by management or those charged with governance to assess the effect of a significant deficiency previously communicated to them and either to correct it or to conclude that it does not need to be corrected.

h. Inadequate controls for the safeguarding of assets.

i. Evidence of intentional override of internal control by those in authority to the detriment of the overall objectives of the system.

j. Deficiencies in the design or operation of internal control that could fail to prevent, or detect and correct, fraud, noncompliance with provisions of laws, regulations, contracts or grant agreements, or abuse having a material effect on the financial statements or the audit objective.

k. Inadequate design of information systems general, application, and user controls that prevent the information system from providing complete and accurate information consistent with financial, compliance, or performance reporting objectives or other current needs.

l. Failure of an application control caused by a deficiency in the design or operation of an information systems general control.

m. Employees or management who lack the qualifications and training to fulfill their assigned functions.

Examples of Abuse

A.07 GAGAS contains requirements for responding to indications of material abuse and reporting abuse that is material to the audit objectives.

a. For financial audits, see paragraphs 4.07 and 4.08 and 4.25 through 4.27.

b. For attestation engagements, see paragraphs 5.08 through 5.09 and 5.24 through 5.26.

c. For performance audits, see paragraphs 6.33 and 6.34 and 7.21 through 7.23.

A.08 The following are examples of abuse, depending on the facts and circumstances:

a. Creating unneeded overtime.

b. Requesting staff to perform personal errands or work tasks for a supervisor or manager.

c. Misusing the official's position for personal gain (including actions that could be perceived by an objective third party with knowledge of the relevant information as improperly benefiting an official's personal financial interests or those of an immediate or close family member; a general partner; an organization for which the official serves as an officer, director, trustee, or employee; or an organization with which the official is negotiating concerning future employment).

d. Making travel choices that are contrary to existing travel policies or are unnecessarily extravagant or expensive.

e. Making procurement or vendor selections that are contrary to existing policies or are unnecessarily extravagant or expensive.

Examples of Indicators of Fraud Risk

A.09 GAGAS contains requirements relating to evaluating fraud risk.

a. For financial audits, see paragraphs 4.06 and 4.25 through 4.27.

b. For attestation engagements, see paragraphs 5.07, 5.20, and 5.24 through 5.26.

c. For performance audits, see paragraphs 6.30 through 6.32 and 7.21 through 7.23.

A.10 In some circumstances, conditions such as the following might indicate a heightened risk of fraud:

a. economic, programmatic, or entity operating conditions threaten the entity's financial stability, viability, or budget;

b. the nature of the entity's operations provide opportunities to engage in fraud;

c. management's monitoring of compliance with policies, laws, and regulations is inadequate;

d. the organizational structure is unstable or unnecessarily complex;

e. communication and/or support for ethical standards by management is lacking;

f. management is willing to accept unusually high levels of risk in making significant decisions;

g. the entity has a history of impropriety, such as previous issues with fraud, waste, abuse, or questionable practices, or past audits or investigations with findings of questionable or criminal activity;

h. operating policies and procedures have not been developed or are outdated;

i. key documentation is lacking or does not exist;

j. asset accountability or safeguarding procedures is lacking;

k. improper payments;

l. false or misleading information;

m. a pattern of large procurements in any budget line with remaining funds at year end, in order to "use up all of the funds available;" and

n. unusual patterns and trends in contracting, procurement, acquisition, and other activities of the entity or program.

Determining Whether Provisions of Laws, Regulations, Contracts and Grant Agreements Are Significant within the Context of the Audit Objectives	**A.11** GAGAS contains requirements for determining whether provisions of laws, regulations, contracts or grant agreements are significant within the context of the audit objectives.

a. For financial audits, see paragraphs 4.19 through 4.22.

b. For attestation engagements, see paragraphs 5.07 and 5.08.

c. For performance audits, see paragraphs 6.28 and 6.29.

A.12 Government programs are subject to many provisions of laws, regulations, contracts or grant agreements. At the same time, their significance within the context of the audit objectives varies widely, depending on the objectives of the audit. Auditors may find the following approach helpful in assessing whether provisions of laws, regulations, contracts or grant agreements are significant within the context of the audit objectives:

a. Express each audit objective in terms of questions about specific aspects of the program being audited (that is, purpose and goals, internal control, inputs, program operations, outputs, and outcomes).

b. Identify provisions of laws, regulations, contracts or grant agreements that directly relate to specific aspects of the program within the context of the audit objectives.

c. Determine if the audit objectives or the auditors' conclusions could be significantly affected if noncompliance with those provisions of laws, regulations, contracts or grant agreements occurred. If the audit objectives or audit conclusions could be significantly affected, then those provisions of laws, regulations, contracts or grant agreements are likely to be significant to the audit objectives.

A.13 Auditors may consult with their own legal counsel to (1) determine those laws and regulations that are significant to the audit objectives, (2) design tests of compliance with laws and regulations, or (3) evaluate the results of those tests. Auditors also may consult with their own legal counsel when audit objectives require testing compliance with provisions of contracts or grant agreements. Depending on the circumstances of the audit, auditors may consult with others, such as investigative staff, other audit organizations or government entities that provided professional services to the audited entity, or applicable law enforcement authorities, to obtain information on compliance matters.

Information to Accompany Chapter 1

A1.01 Chapter 1 discusses the use and application of GAGAS and the role of auditing in government accountability. Those charged with governance and management of audited organizations also have roles in government accountability. The discussion that follows is provided to assist auditors in understanding the roles of others in accountability. The following section also contains background information on the laws, regulations, or other authoritative sources that require the use of GAGAS. This information is provided to place GAGAS within the context of overall government accountability.

Laws, Regulations, and Other Authoritative Sources That Require Use of GAGAS

A1.02 Laws, regulations, contracts, grant agreements, or policies frequently require the use of GAGAS.[176] The following are some of the laws, regulations, and or other authoritative sources that require the use of GAGAS:

a. The Inspector General Act of 1978, as amended, 5 U.S.C. App. requires that the statutorily appointed federal inspectors general comply with GAGAS for audits of federal establishments, organizations, programs, activities, and functions. The act further states that the inspectors general shall take appropriate steps to assure that any work performed by nonfederal auditors complies with GAGAS.

b. The Chief Financial Officers Act of 1990 (Public Law 101-576), as expanded by the Government Management Reform Act of 1994 (Public Law 103-356), requires that GAGAS be followed in audits of executive branch departments' and agencies' financial statements. The Accountability of Tax Dollars Act of 2002 (Public Law 107-289) generally extends this

---

[176]See paragraph 1.06 for additional discussion on the use of GAGAS.

requirement to most executive agencies not subject to the Chief Financial Officers Act unless they are exempted for a given year by the Office of Management and Budget (OMB).

c. The Single Audit Act Amendments of 1996 (Public Law 104-156) require that GAGAS be followed in audits of state and local governments and nonprofit entities that receive federal awards. OMB Circular No. A-133, *Audits of States, Local Governments, and Non-Profit Organizations*, which provides the governmentwide guidelines and policies on performing audits to comply with the Single Audit Act, also requires the use of GAGAS.

A1.03 Other laws, regulations, or authoritative sources may require the use of GAGAS. For example, auditors at the state and local levels of government may be required by state and local laws and regulations to follow GAGAS. Also, auditors may be required by the terms of an agreement or contract to follow GAGAS. Auditors may also be required to follow GAGAS by federal audit guidelines pertaining to program requirements, such as those issued for Housing and Urban Development programs and Student Financial Aid programs. Being alert to such other laws, regulations, or authoritative sources may assist auditors in performing their work in accordance with the required standards.

A1.04 Even if not required to do so, auditors may find it useful to follow GAGAS in performing audits of federal, state, and local government programs as well as audits of government awards administered by contractors, nonprofit entities, and other nongovernmental entities. Many audit organizations not formally required to do so, both in the United States of America and in other countries, voluntarily follow GAGAS.

The Role of Those Charged with Governance

A1.05 During the course of GAGAS audits, auditors communicate with those charged with governance.[177]

a. For financial audits, see paragraphs 4.03 and 4.04.

b. For attestation engagements, see paragraphs 5.04 and 5.05.

c. For performance audits, see paragraphs 6.47 through 6.50.

A1.06 Those charged with governance are responsible for overseeing the strategic direction of the entity and obligations related to the accountability of the entity. This includes overseeing the financial reporting process, subject matter, or program under audit including related internal controls. In certain entities covered by GAGAS, those charged with governance may also be part of the entity's management. In some audit entities, multiple parties may be charged with governance, including oversight bodies, members or staff of legislative committees, boards of directors, audit committees, or parties contracting for the audit.

A1.07 Because the governance structures of government entities and organizations can vary widely, it may not always be clearly evident who is charged with key governance functions. In these situations, auditors evaluate the organizational structure for directing and controlling operations to achieve the audited entity's objectives. This evaluation also includes how the audited entity delegates authority and establishes accountability for its management personnel.

---

[177]See paragraph 1.02 for additional discussion of those charged with governance.

Management's Role

A1.08 Managers have fundamental responsibilities for carrying out government functions.[178] Management of the audited entity is responsible for

a. using its financial, physical, and informational resources legally, effectively, efficiently, economically, ethically, and equitably to achieve the purposes for which the resources were furnished or the program was established;

b. complying with applicable laws and regulations (including identifying the requirements with which the entity and the official are responsible for compliance);

c. implementing systems designed to achieve compliance with applicable laws and regulations;

d. establishing and maintaining effective internal control to help ensure that appropriate goals and objectives are met; following laws and regulations; and ensuring that management and financial information is reliable and properly reported;

e. providing appropriate reports to those who oversee their actions and to the public in order to demonstrate accountability for the resources and authority used to carry out government programs and the results of these programs;

f. addressing the findings and recommendations of auditors, and for establishing and maintaining a process to track the status of such findings and recommendations;

---

[178]See paragraphs 1.01 and 1.02 for additional discussion of management and officials of government programs.

g. following sound procurement practices when contracting for audits, including ensuring procedures are in place for monitoring contract performance; and

h. taking timely and appropriate steps to remedy fraud, noncompliance with provisions of laws, regulations, contracts or grant agreements, or abuse that auditors report.

Information to Accompany Chapter 2

Attestation Engagements

A2.01 Examples of attestation engagements objectives[179] include

a. prospective financial or performance information;

b. management's discussion and analysis (MD&A) presentation;

c. an entity's internal control over financial reporting;

d. the effectiveness of an entity's internal control over compliance with specified requirements, such as those governing the bidding for, accounting for, and reporting on grants and contracts;

e. an entity's compliance with requirements of specified laws, regulations, policies, contracts, or grants;

f. the accuracy and reliability of reported performance measures;

---

[179]See paragraph 2.09 for additional discussion of attestation engagements.

g. whether incurred final contract costs are supported with required evidence and in compliance with the contract terms;

h. the allowability and reasonableness of proposed contract amounts that are based on detailed costs; and

i. the quantity, condition, or valuation of inventory or assets.

Performance Audit Objectives	**A2.02** Examples of program effectiveness and results audit objectives[180] include:

a. assessing the extent to which legislative, regulatory, or organizational goals and objectives are being achieved;

b. assessing the relative ability of alternative approaches to yield better program performance or eliminate factors that inhibit program effectiveness;

c. analyzing the relative cost-effectiveness of a program or activity, focusing on combining cost information or other inputs with information about outputs or the benefit provided or with outcomes or the results achieved;

d. determining whether a program produced intended results or produced results that were not consistent with the program's objectives;

e. determining the current status or condition of program operations or progress in implementing legislative requirements;

---

[180]See paragraph 2.11a for additional discussion of program effectiveness and results audit objectives.

f. determining whether a program provides equitable access to or distribution of public resources within the context of statutory parameters;

g. assessing the extent to which programs duplicate, overlap, or conflict with other related programs;

h. evaluating whether the entity is following sound procurement practices;

i. assessing the reliability, validity, or relevance of performance measures concerning program effectiveness and results, or economy and efficiency;

j. assessing the reliability, validity, or relevance of financial information related to the performance of a program;

k. determining whether government resources (inputs) are obtained at reasonable costs while meeting timeliness and quality considerations;

l. determining whether appropriate value was obtained based on the cost or amount paid or based on the amount of revenue received;

m. determining whether government services and benefits are accessible to those individuals who have a right to access those services and benefits;

n. determining whether fees assessed cover costs;

o. determining whether and how the program's unit costs can be decreased or its productivity increased; and

p. assessing the reliability, validity, or relevance of budget proposals or budget requests to assist legislatures in the budget process.

A2.03 Examples of audit objectives related to internal control[181] include an assessment of the extent to which internal control provides reasonable assurance about whether

a. organizational missions, goals, and objectives are achieved effectively and efficiently;

b. resources are used in compliance with laws, regulations, or other requirements;

c. resources, including sensitive information accessed or stored outside the organization's physical perimeter, are safeguarded against unauthorized acquisition, use, or disposition;

d. management information, such as performance measures, and public reports are complete, accurate, and consistent to support performance and decision making;

e. the integrity of information from computerized systems is achieved; and

f. contingency planning for information systems provides essential back-up to prevent unwarranted disruption of the activities and functions that the systems support.

A2.04 Compliance objectives[182] include determining whether

---

[181]See paragraph 2.11b for additional discussion of internal control audit objectives.

[182]See paragraph 2.11c for additional discussion of compliance audit objectives.

a. the purpose of the program, the manner in which it is to be conducted, the services delivered, the outcomes, or the population it serves is in compliance with provisions of laws, regulations, contracts or grant agreements, or other requirements;

b. government services and benefits are distributed or delivered to citizens based on the individual's eligibility to obtain those services and benefits;

c. incurred or proposed costs are in compliance with applicable laws, regulations, contracts, or grant agreements; and

d. revenues received are in compliance with applicable laws, regulations, contracts or grant agreements.

A2.05 Examples of objectives pertaining to prospective analysis[183] include providing conclusions based on

a. current and projected trends and future potential impact on government programs and services;

b. program or policy alternatives, including forecasting program outcomes under various assumptions;

c. policy or legislative proposals, including advantages, disadvantages, and analysis of stakeholder views;

d. prospective information prepared by management;

e. budgets and forecasts that are based on (1) assumptions about expected future events and (2) management's expected reaction to those future events; and

---

[183]See paragraph 2.11d for additional discussion of prospective analysis audit objectives.

f. management's assumptions on which prospective
information is based.

**GAGAS Compliance
Statements**

A2.06 The determination of whether an unmodified or
modified GAGAS compliance statement is appropriate
is based on the consideration of the individual and
aggregate effect of exceptions to GAGAS
requirements.[184] Quantitative and qualitative factors that
the auditor may consider include:

a. the likelihood that the exception(s) will affect the
perceptions of report users about the audit findings,
conclusions, and recommendations;

b. the magnitude of the effect of the exception(s) on the
perceptions of report users about the audit findings,
conclusions, and recommendations;

c. the pervasiveness of the exception(s);

d. the potential effect of the exception(s) on the
sufficiency and appropriateness of evidence supporting
the audit findings, conclusions, and recommendations;
and

e. whether report users could be misled if the GAGAS
compliance statement were not modified.

**Information to
Accompany
Chapter 3**

A3.01 Chapter 3 discusses the general standards
applicable to financial audits, attestation engagements,
and performance audits in accordance with GAGAS.
The following supplemental guidance is provided to
assist auditors and audited entities in avoiding

---

[184]See paragraphs 2.24 and 2.25 for additional discussion on citing
compliance with GAGAS.

impairments to independence, establishing a system of quality control, and identifying peer review risk factors.

Threats to Independence

A3.02 This list is intended to illustrate by example the types of circumstances that create threats to independence that an auditor might identify when applying the conceptual framework.[185] It does not include all circumstances that create threats to independence; these circumstances will be unique to the conditions under which each evaluation takes place.

A3.03 Examples of circumstances that create self-interest threats for an auditor include:

a. A member of the audit team having a direct financial interest in the audited entity. This would not preclude auditors from auditing pension plans that they participate in if (1) the auditor has no control over the investment strategy, benefits, or other management issues associated with the pension plan and (2) the auditor belongs to such pension plan as part of his/her employment with the audit organization, provided that the plan is normally offered to all employees in equivalent employment positions.

b. An audit organization having undue dependence on income from a particular audited entity.

c. A member of the audit team entering into employment negotiations with an audited entity.

d. An auditor discovering a significant error when evaluating the results of a previous professional service performed by a member of the auditor's audit organization.

---

[185]See paragraphs 3.07 through 3.26.

A3.04 Examples of circumstances that create self-review threats for an auditor include:

a. An audit organization issuing a report on the effectiveness of the operation of financial or performance management systems after designing or implementing the systems.

b. An audit organization having prepared the original data used to generate records that are the subject matter of the audit.

c. An audit organization performing a service for an audited entity that directly affects the subject matter information of the audit.

d. A member of the audit team being, or having recently been, employed by the audited entity in a position to exert significant influence over the subject matter of the audit.

A3.05 Examples of circumstances that create bias threats for an auditor include:

a. An auditor's having preconceptions about the objectives of a program under audit that are sufficiently strong to impact the auditor's objectivity.

b. An auditor's having biases associated with political, ideological, or social convictions that result from membership or employment in, or loyalty to, a particular type of policy, group, organization, or level of government that could impact the auditor's objectivity.

A3.06 Examples of circumstances that create familiarity threats for an auditor include:

a. A member of the audit team having a close or immediate family member who is a principal or senior manager of the audited entity.

b. A member of the audit team having a close or immediate family member who is an employee of the audited entity and is in a position to exert significant influence over the subject matter of the audit.

c. A principal or employee of the audited entity in a position to exert significant influence over the subject matter of the audit having recently served on the audit team.

d. An auditor accepting gifts or preferential treatment from an audited entity, unless the value is trivial or inconsequential.

e. Senior audit personnel having a long association with the audited entity.

A3.07 Examples of circumstances that create undue influence threats for an auditor or audit organization include existence of:

a. External interference or influence that could improperly limit or modify the scope of an audit or threaten to do so, including exerting pressure to inappropriately reduce the extent of work performed in order to reduce costs or fees.

b. External interference with the selection or application of audit procedures or in the selection of transactions to be examined.

c. Unreasonable restrictions on the time allowed to complete an audit or issue the report.

d. External interference over the assignment, appointment, compensation, and promotion of audit personnel.

e. Restrictions on funds or other resources provided to the audit organization that adversely affect the audit organization's ability to carry out its responsibilities.

f. Authority to overrule or to inappropriately influence the auditors' judgment as to the appropriate content of the report.

g. Threat of replacing the auditors over a disagreement with the contents of an auditors' report, the auditors' conclusions, or the application of an accounting principle or other criteria.

h. Influences that jeopardize the auditors' continued employment for reasons other than incompetence, misconduct, or the need for audits or attestation engagements.

A3.08 Examples of circumstances that create management participation threats for an auditor include:

a. A member of the audit team being, or having recently been, a principal or senior manager of the audited entity.

b. An audit organization principal or employee serving as a voting member of an entity's management committee or board of directors, making policy decisions that affect future direction and operation of an entity's programs, supervising entity employees, developing or approving programmatic policy, authorizing an entity's transactions, or maintaining custody of an entity's assets.

c. An audit organization principal or employee recommending a single individual for a specific position that is key to the entity or program under audit, or otherwise ranking or influencing management's selection of the candidate.

d. An auditor preparing management's corrective action plan to deal with deficiencies detected in the audit.

A3.09 Examples of circumstances that create structural threats for an auditor include:

a. For both external and internal audit organizations, structural placement of the audit function within the reporting line of the areas under audit.

b. For internal audit organizations, administrative direction from the audited entity's management.

System of Quality Control

A3.10 Chapter 3 discusses the elements of an audit organization's system of quality control.[186] The following supplemental guidance is provided to assist auditors and audit organizations in establishing policies and procedures in its system of quality control to address the following elements: initiation, acceptance, and continuance of audits; audit performance, documentation, and reporting; and monitoring.

a. Government audit organizations initiate audits as a result of (1) legal mandates, (2) requests from legislative bodies or oversight bodies, and (3) the audit organization's discretion. In the case of legal mandates and requests, a government audit organization may be required to perform the audit and may not be permitted

---

[186]See paragraphs 3.82 through 3.95 for additional discussion of the system of quality control.

to make decisions about acceptance or continuance and may not be permitted to resign or withdraw from the audit.

b. GAGAS standards for audit performance, documentation, and reporting are in chapter 4 for financial audits, chapter 5 for attestation engagements, and chapters 6 and 7 for performance audits. Chapter 3 specifies that an audit organization's quality control system include policies and procedures designed to provide the audit organization with reasonable assurance that audits are performed and reports are issued in accordance with professional standards and legal and regulatory requirements.[187] Examples of such policies and procedures include the following:

(1) communication provided to team members so that they sufficiently understand the objectives of their work and the applicable professional standards;

(2) audit planning and supervision;

(3) appropriate documentation of the work performed;

(4) review of the work performed, the significant judgments made, and the resulting audit documentation and report;

(5) review of the independence and qualifications of any external specialists or contractors used, as well as a review of the scope and quality of their work;

(6) procedures for resolving difficult or contentious issues or disagreements among team members, including specialists;

---

[187]See paragraphs 3.82 through 3.95 for additional discussion of quality control policies and procedures.

(7) obtaining and addressing comments from the audited entity on draft reports; and

(8) reporting supported by the evidence obtained, and in accordance with applicable professional standards and legal or regulatory requirements.

c. Monitoring is an ongoing, periodic assessment of audits designed to provide management of the audit organization with reasonable assurance that the policies and procedures related to the system of quality control are suitably designed and operating effectively in practice.[188] The following guidance is provided to assist audit organizations with implementing and continuing its monitoring of quality:

(1) Who: Monitoring is most effective when performed by persons who do not have responsibility for the specific activity being monitored (e.g., for specific audits or specific centralized processes). The staff member or team of staff members assigned with responsibility for the monitoring process collectively need sufficient and appropriate competence and authority in the audit organization to assume that responsibility. Generally the staff member or the team of staff members performing the monitoring are apart from the normal audit supervision associated with individual audits.

(2) How much: The extent of monitoring procedures varies based on the audit organization's circumstances to enable the audit organization to assess compliance with applicable professional standards and the audit organization's quality control policies and procedures. Examples of specific monitoring procedures include

---

[188]See paragraphs 3.93 through 3.95 for additional discussion of monitoring.

(a) examination of selected administrative and personnel records pertaining to quality control;

(b) review of selected audit documentation and reports;

(c) discussions with the audit organization's personnel (as applicable and appropriate);

(d) periodic summarization of the findings from the monitoring procedures in writing (at least annually), and consideration of the systematic causes of findings that indicate improvements are needed;

(e) determination of any corrective actions to be taken or improvements to be made with respect to the specific audits reviewed or the audit organization's quality control policies and procedures;

(f) communication of the identified findings to appropriate audit organization management with subsequent follow-up; and

(g) consideration of findings by appropriate audit organization management personnel who also determine whether actions necessary, Including necessary modifications to the quality control system, are performed on a timely basis.

(3) Review of selected administrative and personnel records: The review of selected administrative and personnel records pertaining to quality control may include tests of

(a) compliance with policies and procedures on independence;

(b) compliance with continuing professional development policies, including training;

(c) procedures related to recruitment and hiring of qualified personnel, including hiring of specialists or consultants when needed;

(d) procedures related to performance evaluation and advancement of personnel;

(e) procedures related to initiation, acceptance, and continuance of audits;

(f) audit organization personnel's understanding of the quality control policies and procedures, and implementation of these policies and procedures; and

(g) audit organization's process for updating its policies and procedures.

(4) Follow-up on previous findings: Monitoring procedures include an evaluation of whether the audit organization has taken appropriate corrective action to address findings and recommendations from previous monitoring and peer reviews. Personnel involved in monitoring use this information as part of the assessment of risk associated with the design and implementation of the audit organization's quality control system and in determining the nature, timing, and extent of monitoring procedures.

(5) Communication: The audit organization communicates internally the results of the monitoring of its quality control systems that allows the audit organization to take prompt and appropriate action where necessary. Information included in this communication includes:

(a) a description of the monitoring procedures performed;

(b) the conclusions drawn from the monitoring procedures; and

(c) where relevant, a description of the systemic, repetitive, or other significant deficiencies and of the actions taken to resolve those deficiencies.

Peer Review

A3.11 Examples of the factors to consider when performing an assessment of peer review risk for selecting audits for peer review[189] include:

a. scope of the audits including size of the audited entity or audits covering multiple locations;

b. functional area or type of government program;

c. types of audits provided, including the extent of nonaudit services provided to audited entities;

d. personnel (including use of new personnel or personnel not routinely assigned the types of audits provided);

e. initial audits;

f. familiarity resulting from a longstanding relationship with the audited entity;

g. political sensitivity of the audits;

h. budget constraints for the audit organization;

i. results of the peer review team's review of the design of system of quality control;

---

[189]See paragraph 3.99 for additional discussion of the assessment of peer review risk.

j. results of the audit organization's monitoring process; and

k. risk sensitivity of the audit organization.

A3.12 As discussed in paragraph 3.105, an external audit organization should make its most recent peer review report publicly available. Examples of how to achieve this transparency requirement include posting the peer review report on an external Web site or to a publicly available file. To help the public understand the peer review reports, an audit organization may also include a description of the peer review process and how it applies to its organization. The following provides examples of additional information that audit organizations may include to help users understand the meaning of the peer review report.

a. Explanation of the peer review process.

b. Description of the audit organization's system of quality control.

c. Explanation of the relationship of the peer review results to the audited organization's work.

d. If the peer review report that includes deficiencies or significant deficiencies is modified, explanation of the reviewed audit organization's plan for improving quality controls and the status of the improvements.

Information to Accompany Chapter 6

A6.01 Chapter 6 discusses the field work standards for performance audits. An integral concept for performance auditing is the use of sufficient, appropriate evidence based on the audit objectives to support a sound basis for audit findings, conclusions, and recommendations. The following discussion is provided to assist auditors in identifying criteria and the various types of evidence, including assessing the appropriateness of evidence in relation to the audit objectives.

Types of Criteria

A6.02 The following are some examples of criteria:[190]

a. purpose or goals prescribed by law or regulation or set by officials of the audited entity,

b. policies and procedures established by officials of the audited entity,

c. technically developed standards or norms,

d. expert opinions,

e. prior periods' performance,

f. defined business practices,

g. contract or grant terms, and

h. performance of other entities or sectors used as defined benchmarks.

A6.03 Audit objectives may pertain to describing the current status or condition of a program or process. For this type of audit objective, criteria may also be represented by the assurance added by the auditor's (1) description of the status or condition, (2) evaluation of whether the status or condition meets certain characteristics, or (3) evaluation of whether management's description is verifiable, accurate, or supported.

---

[190]See paragraph 6.37 for additional discussion on identifying audit criteria.

Types of Evidence

A6.04 In terms of its form and how it is collected, evidence may be categorized as physical, documentary, or testimonial. Physical evidence is obtained by auditors' direct inspection or observation of people, property, or events. Such evidence may be documented in summary memos, photographs, videos, drawings, charts, maps, or physical samples. Documentary evidence is obtained in the form of already existing information such as letters, contracts, accounting records, invoices, spreadsheets, database extracts, electronically stored information, and management information on performance. Testimonial evidence is obtained through inquiries, interviews, focus groups, public forums, or questionnaires. Auditors frequently use analytical processes including computations, comparisons, separation of information into components, and rational arguments to analyze any evidence gathered to determine whether it is sufficient and appropriate.[191] The strength and weakness of each form of evidence depends on the facts and circumstances associated with the evidence and professional judgment in the context of the audit objectives.

Appropriateness of Evidence in Relation to the Audit Objectives

A6.05 One of the primary factors influencing the assurance associated with a performance audit is the appropriateness of the evidence in relation to the audit objectives.[192] For example:

a. The audit objectives might focus on verifying specific quantitative results presented by the audited entity. In these situations, the audit procedures would likely focus

---

[191]See paragraphs 6.67 and 6.60 for definitions of sufficient and appropriate.

[192]See paragraphs 6.60 through 6.66 for additional discussion on the appropriateness of evidence.

on obtaining evidence about the accuracy of the specific amounts in question. This work may include the use of statistical sampling.

b. The audit objectives might focus on the performance of a specific program or activity in the agency being audited. In these situations, the auditor may be provided with information compiled by the agency being audited in order to answer the audit objectives. The auditor may find it necessary to test the quality of the information, which includes both its validity and reliability.

c. The audit objectives might focus on information that is used for widely accepted purposes and obtained from sources generally recognized as appropriate. For example, economic statistics issued by government agencies for purposes such as adjusting for inflation, or other such information issued by authoritative organizations, may be the best information available. In such cases, it may not be practical or necessary for auditors to conduct procedures to verify the information. These decisions call for professional judgment based on the nature of the information, its common usage or acceptance, and how it is being used in the audit.

d. The audit objectives might focus on comparisons or benchmarking between various government functions or agencies. These types of audits are especially useful for analyzing the outcomes of various public policy decisions. In these cases, auditors may perform analyses, such as comparative statistics of different jurisdictions or changes in performance over time, where it would be impractical to verify the detailed data underlying the statistics. Clear disclosure as to what extent the comparative information or statistics were evaluated or corroborated will likely be necessary to place the evidence in context for report users.

e. The audit objectives might focus on trend information based on data provided by the audited entity. In this situation, auditors may assess the evidence by using overall analytical tests of underlying data, combined with a knowledge and understanding of the systems or processes used for compiling information.

f. The audit objectives might focus on the auditor identifying emerging and cross-cutting issues using information compiled or self-reported by agencies. In such cases, it may be helpful for the auditor to consider the overall appropriateness of the compiled information along with other information available about the program. Other sources of information, such as inspector general reports or other external audits, may provide the auditors with information regarding whether any unverified or self-reported information is consistent with or can be corroborated by these other external sources of information.

Findings

A6.06 When the audit objectives include explaining why a particular type of positive or negative program performance, output, or outcome identified in the audit occurred, they are referred to as "cause."[193] Identifying the cause of problems may assist auditors in making constructive recommendations for correction. Because deficiencies can result from a number of plausible factors or multiple causes, the recommendation can be more persuasive if auditors can clearly demonstrate and explain with evidence and reasoning the link between the deficiencies and the factor or factors they have identified as the cause or causes. Auditors may also identify deficiencies in program design or structure as the cause of deficient performance. Auditors may also identify deficiencies in internal control that are

---

[193]See paragraph 6.76 for additional discussion of "cause."

significant to the subject matter of the performance audit as the cause of deficient performance. In developing these types of findings, the deficiencies in program design or internal control would be described as the "cause." Often the causes of deficient program performance are complex and involve multiple factors, including fundamental, systemic root causes. Alternatively, when the audit objectives include estimating the program's effect on changes in physical, social, or economic conditions, auditors seek evidence of the extent to which the program itself is the "cause" of those changes.

A6.07 When the audit objectives include estimating the extent to which a program has caused changes in physical, social, or economic conditions, "effect" is a measure of the impact achieved by the program. In this case, "effect" is the extent to which positive or negative changes in actual physical, social, or economic conditions can be identified and attributed to the program.

Information to Accompany Chapter 7

A7.01 Chapter 7 discusses the reporting standards for performance audits. The following discussion is provided to assist auditors in developing and writing their audit report for performance audits.

Report Quality Elements

A7.02 The auditor may use the report quality elements of timely, complete, accurate, objective, convincing, clear, and concise when developing and writing the audit report as the subject permits.[194]

a. Accurate: An accurate report is supported by sufficient, appropriate evidence with key facts, figures,

---

[194]See paragraph 7.08 for additional discussion of report contents.

and findings being traceable to the audit evidence. Reports that are fact-based, with a clear statement of sources, methods, and assumptions so that report users can judge how much weight to give the evidence reported, assist in achieving accuracy. Disclosing data limitations and other disclosures also contribute to producing more accurate audit reports. Reports also are more accurate when the findings are presented in the broader context of the issue. One way to help audit organizations prepare accurate audit reports is to use a quality control process such as referencing. Referencing is a process in which an experienced auditor who is independent of the audit checks that statements of facts, figures, and dates are correctly reported, that the findings are adequately supported by the evidence in the audit documentation, and that the conclusions and recommendations flow logically from the evidence.

b. Objective: Objective means that the presentation of the report is balanced in content and tone. A report's credibility is significantly enhanced when it presents evidence in an unbiased manner and in the proper context. This means presenting the audit results impartially and fairly. The tone of reports may encourage decision makers to act on the auditors' findings and recommendations. This balanced tone can be achieved when reports present sufficient, appropriate evidence to support conclusions while refraining from using adjectives or adverbs that characterize evidence in a way that implies criticism or unsupported conclusions. The objectivity of audit reports is enhanced when the report explicitly states the source of the evidence and the assumptions used in the analysis. The report may recognize the positive aspects of the program reviewed if applicable to the audit objectives. Inclusion of positive program aspects may lead to improved performance by other government organizations that read the report. Audit reports are more objective when they demonstrate that the work has been performed by professional, unbiased, independent, and knowledgeable staff.

c. Complete: Being complete means that the report contains sufficient, appropriate evidence needed to satisfy the audit objectives and promote an understanding of the matters reported. It also means the report states evidence and findings without omission of significant relevant information related to the audit objectives. Providing report users with an understanding means providing perspective on the extent and significance of reported findings, such as the frequency of occurrence relative to the number of cases or transactions tested and the relationship of the findings to the entity's operations. Being complete also means clearly stating what was and was not done and explicitly describing data limitations, constraints imposed by restrictions on access to records, or other issues.

d. Convincing: Being convincing means that the audit results are responsive to the audit objectives, that the findings are presented persuasively, and that the conclusions and recommendations flow logically from the facts presented. The validity of the findings, the reasonableness of the conclusions, and the benefit of implementing the recommendations are more convincing when supported by sufficient, appropriate evidence. Reports designed in this way can help focus the attention of responsible officials on the matters that warrant attention and can provide an incentive for taking corrective action.

e. Clear: Clarity means the report is easy for the intended user to read and understand. Preparing the report in language as clear and simple as the subject permits assists auditors in achieving this goal. Use of straightforward, nontechnical language is helpful to simplify presentation. Defining technical terms, abbreviations, and acronyms that are used in the report is also helpful. Auditors may use a highlights page or summary within the report to capture the report user's attention and highlight the overall message. If a summary is used, it is helpful if it focuses on the specific answers to the questions in the audit objectives, summarizes the audit's most significant findings and the report's principal conclusions, and prepares users to anticipate the major recommendations. Logical organization of material, and accuracy and precision in stating facts and in drawing conclusions assist in the report's clarity and understanding. Effective use of titles and captions and topic sentences makes the report easier to read and understand. Visual aids (such as pictures, charts, graphs, and maps) may clarify and summarize complex material.

f. Concise: Being concise means that the report is not longer than necessary to convey and support the message. Extraneous detail detracts from a report, may even conceal the real message, and may confuse or distract the users. Although room exists for considerable judgment in determining the content of reports, those that are fact-based but concise are likely to achieve results.

g. Timely: To be of maximum use, providing relevant evidence in time to respond to officials of the audited entity, legislative officials, and other users' legitimate needs is the auditors' goal. Likewise, the evidence provided in the report is more helpful if it is current. Therefore, the timely issuance of the report is an important reporting goal for auditors. During the audit, the auditors may provide interim reports of significant matters to appropriate entity officials. Such communication alerts officials to matters needing immediate attention and allows them to take corrective action before the final report is completed.

GAGAS Conceptual Framework for Independence

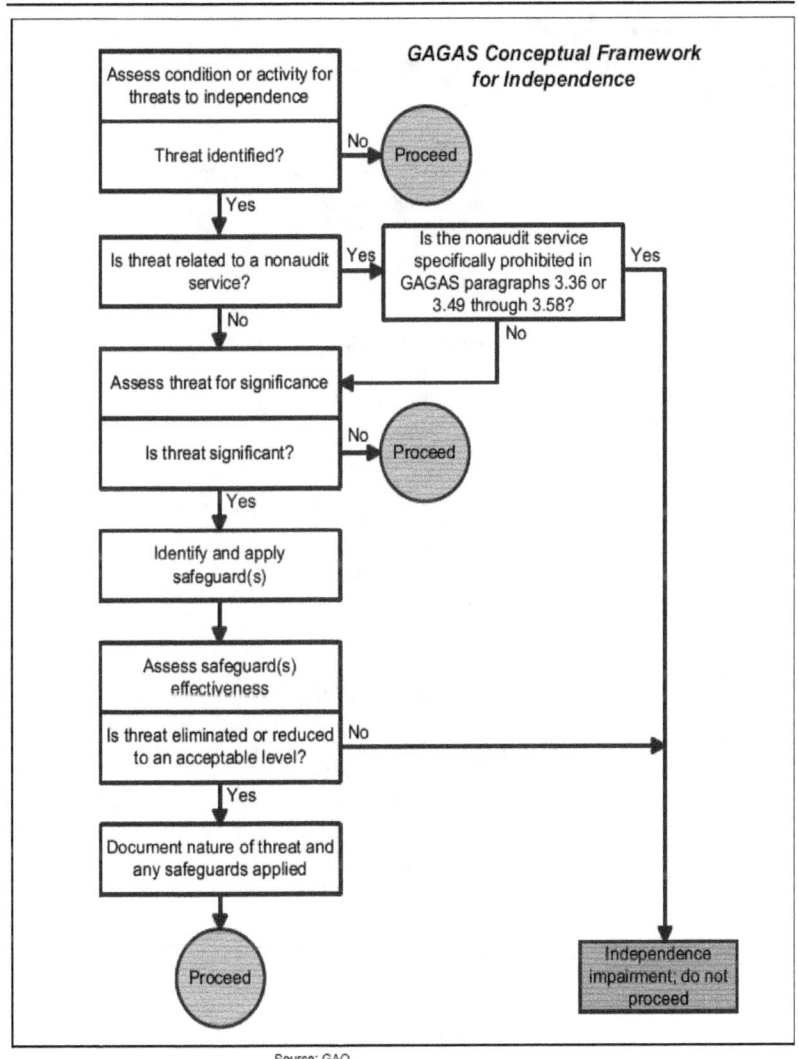

GAGAS Conceptual Framework for Independence

Assess condition or activity for threats to independence

Threat identified? — No → Proceed

Yes ↓

Is threat related to a nonaudit service? — Yes → Is the nonaudit service specifically prohibited in GAGAS paragraphs 3.36 or 3.49 through 3.58? — Yes →

No ↓   No ↓

Assess threat for significance

Is threat significant? — No → Proceed

Yes ↓

Identify and apply safeguard(s)

Assess safeguard(s) effectiveness

Is threat eliminated or reduced to an acceptable level? — No →

Yes ↓

Document nature of threat and any safeguards applied

Proceed

Independence impairment; do not proceed

Source: GAO.

Comptroller General's Advisory Council on Government Auditing Standards

Advisory Council Members	Auston Johnson, Chair State of Utah (2009-2011)
	The Honorable Ernest A. Almonte State of Rhode Island (member 2005-2008)
	Christine C. Boesz Consultant (member 2007-2011)
	Kathy A. Buller Peace Corps (member 2009-2011)
	Dr. Paul A. Copley James Madison University (member 2005-2008)
	David Cotton Cotton & Co. LLP (member 2006-2009)
	Beryl H. Davis Institute of Internal Auditors (member 2007-2011)
	Kristine Devine Deloitte & Touche, LLP (member 2005-2011)
	Dr. Ehsan Feroz University of Minnesota Duluth (member 2002-2009)

Alex Fraser
Standard & Poor's
(member 2006-2008)

Mark Funkhouser
Kansas City, Missouri
(member 2005-2008)

Dr. Michael H. Granof
University of Texas at Austin
(member 2005-2008)

Jerome Heer
County of Milwaukee, Wisconsin
(member 2004-2011)

Michael Hendricks
Consultant
(member 2010-2012)

Marion Higa
State of Hawaii
(member 2006-2009)

The Honorable John P. Higgins, Jr.
U.S. Department of Education
(member 2005-2008)

Julia Higgs
Florida Atlantic University
(member 2009-2011)

Russell Hinton
State of Georgia
(member 2004-2011)

Drummond Kahn
City of Portland, Oregon
(member 2009-2011)

Richard A. Leach
United States Navy
(member 2005-2011)

David W. Martin
State of Florida
(member 2010-2012)

Patrick L. McNamee
PricewaterhouseCoopers, LLP
(member 2005-2008)

John R. Miller
KPMG LLP (Retired)
(chair 2001-2008)

Nancy A. Miller
Miller Foley Group
(member 2010-2012)

Rakesh Mohan
State of Idaho
(member 2004-2011)

The Honorable Samuel Mok
Consultant
(member 2006-2009)

Harold L. Monk, Jr.
Davis, Monk & Company
(member 2002-2012)

Stephen L. Morgan
City of Austin, Texas
(member 2001-2008)

Janice Mueller
State of Wisconsin
(member 2009-2011)

George A. Rippey
U.S. Department of Education
(member 2010-2012)

The Honorable Jon T. Rymer
Federal Deposit Insurance Corporation
(member 2009-2011)

Brian A. Schebler
McGladrey & Pullen, LLP
(member 2005-2011)

Barry R. Snyder
Federal Reserve Board
(member 2001-2008)

Dr. Daniel L. Stufflebeam
Western Michigan University
(member 2002-2009)

F. Michael Taylor
City of Stockton, California
(member 2010-2012)

Roland L. Unger
State of Maryland
(member 2010)

Edward J. Valenzuela
State of Florida
(member 2007-2009)

Thomas E. Vermeer
Alfred Lerner College of Business & Economics
(member 2010-2012)

Sandra H. Vice
State of Texas
(member 2010-2012)

John C. Weber
Crowe Horwath LLP
(member 2010-2012)

George Willie
Bert Smith & Co.
(member 2004-2011)

GAO Project Team

Jeanette M. Franzel, Managing Director
James R. Dalkin, Project Director
Robert F. Dacey, Chief Accountant
Marcia B. Buchanan, Assistant Director
Cheryl E. Clark, Assistant Director
Heather I. Keister, Assistant Director
Kristen A. Kociolek, Assistant Director
Michael C. Hrapsky, Specialist, Auditing Standards
Eric H. Holbrook, Specialist, Auditing Standards
Maria Hasan, Auditor
Laura S. Pacheco, Auditor
Christie A. Pugnetti, Auditor
Margaret A. Mills, Senior Communications Analyst
Jennifer V. Allison, Council Administrator

Index

abuse (*see also* attestation engagements, field work; attestation engagements, reporting; financial audits, performing; financial audits, reporting; performance audits, field work, performance audits, reporting) A.07-A.08

examples of A.08

accountability

governance, role of those charged with A1.05–A1.07

government 1.01–1.02

government managers and officials, responsibilities of 1.02, A1.08

accurate, as report quality element A7.02

Advisory Council on Government Auditing Standards, members of Appendix III

agreed-upon procedures (*see* attestation engagements)

AICPA standards

for attestation engagements 2.09, 3.74, 4.21, 5.01, 5.02, 5.03, 5.04, 5.07, 5.16, 5.18, 5.19, 5.22, 5.42, 5.46, 5.48, 5.50, 5.51, 5.54, 5.56, 5.57, 5.58, 5.59*fn*, 5.60, 5.61, 5.64, 5.66, 5.67

for financial audits 2.08, 4.01, 4.02, 4.03, 4.06, 4.15, 4.17, 4.18, 4.19, 4.24, 4.47

relationship to GAGAS 2.20a

American Evaluation Association 2.21b

American Institute of Certified Public Accountants (*see also* AICPA standards) 2.20a

American Psychological Association 2.21d

appropriateness of evidence 6.57, 6.60-6.66, A6.05

assurance (*see* quality control and assurance; reasonable assurance)

attestation engagements (*see also* GAGAS)

qualifications for auditors, additional 3.74, 3.75

types of 2.09

subject matter 2.09

attestation engagements

examination engagements, fieldwork 5.03-5.17

additional fieldwork requirements 5.03-5.17

auditor communication 5.04-5.05

developing elements of a finding 5.11-5.15

documentation 5.16-5.17

fraud, noncompliance with provisions of laws, regulations, contracts, and grant agreements 5.07–5.10

previous audits and attestation engagements 5.06

examination engagements, reporting 5.18-5.47

additional considerations, other 5.45-5.47

additional reporting requirements 5.18

attestation engagement 2.09

compliance 2.11c

economy and efficiency 2.11a

information appropriate to A6.01

internal control 2.11b

multiple or overlapping 2.11

performance audit 2.10, 2.11, 6.03, 6.07-6.08

program effectiveness and results 2.11a

prospective analysis 2.11d

types of 2.02-2.11

objective, as report quality element A7.02b

objectives, scope, and methodology (*see also* performance audit, field work and performance audit, reporting) 7.09–7.13

objectivity (*see also* auditors' responsibilities; independence) 1.14c, 1.19

operational audits (*see* performance audits)

peer review, external 3.82b, 3.96-3.107

contracting parties, providing reports to 3.106

public transparency 3.105

risk assessment 3.99

scope 3.96-3.98, 3.102

reporting 3.97, 3.100-3.103

selecting engagements 3.99

team criteria 3.104

work of another audit organization, using 3.107

performance audits (*see* also evidence)

audit objectives, types of 2.11, A2.02-A2.05

definition 2.10

GAGAS and other standards 2.21

performance audits, field work 6.01–6.85

abuse 6.33–6.34

audit plan, preparing 6.51–6.52

audit risk 6.01, 6.05, 6.07, 6.10–6.11, 6.29, 6.36

cause 6.76

communication, auditor 6.47–6.50

compliance objectives 6.19c, A2.04

condition 6.75

www.ingramcontent.com/pod-product-compliance
Lightning Source LLC
Chambersburg PA
CBHW051450170526
45166CB00001B/193